CORY JANE
WINGING IT

CORY JANE
WINGING IT
RANDOM TALES FROM THE RIGHT WING

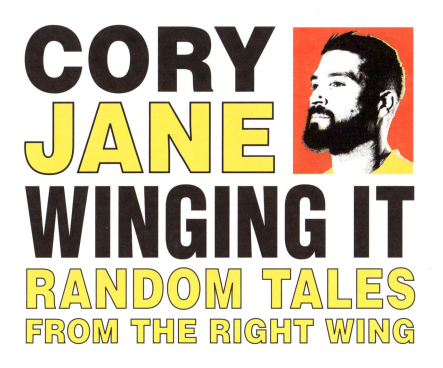

WITH SCOTTY STEVENSON

mower

A catalogue record for this book is available from the
National Library of New Zealand

ISBN 978-1-927262-07-8

A Mower Book
Published in 2015 by Upstart Press Ltd
B3, 72 Apollo Drive, Rosedale
Auckland, New Zealand

Reprinted 2015

Text © Cory Jane 2015
The moral rights of the author have been asserted

Design and format © Upstart Press Ltd 2015

All rights reserved. No part of this publication may be reproduced or transmitted in any form or by any means, electronic or mechanical, including photocopying, recording, or any information storage and retrieval system, without permission in writing from the publisher.

Designed by www.CVDgraphics.nz
Printed by Everbest Printing Co. Ltd., China
Front cover photos: Getty
Back cover illustration: Murray Webb

To my wife Amie, thank you for all the hard work you do behind the scenes to help me reach my goals and achieve my dreams. The fact you raise four crazy kids who are just like their daddy makes you my hero!

To the lads, no hard feelings boys — it's just a little fun.

PS. I have a few more stories in my back pocket. Just in case we need a part two.

CONTENTS

Writer's note   11
Foreword by Israel Dagg   13

1   More Tarzan than Jane   15
2   Falling for the game   29
3   Going Sevens & going Super   49
4   Fulfilling a promise   67
5   To test match rugby & beyond   85
6   On with the job   99
7   Winging it & the rise of the Bomb Squad   113
8   Fashion & tans   131
9   Roomies I have known   143
10   A little tournament at home   161
11   A night to regret   175
12   Old foes & monkeys off backs   185
13   A week of it   197

Epilogue   223

YOu aRe NoW ENtERiNg ThE TWiLIGHT ZoNE

WRITER'S NOTE

I LOVE A GOOD STORY — I always have. So when I was asked to help Cory put his on paper, I jumped at the chance. Cory has stories alright, and a great zest for telling them. Whether he has any friends left after telling them in the following pages is another matter.

We all know Cory is a jokester, but that is a mask that hides a passionate and dedicated footballer who has worked hard to become a world-champion All Black. He has gifts — a great fend, an excellent step, a nose for the tryline — but of all his gifts, his greatest may be his ability to see the funny side of the serious business of professional rugby.

He is a master of self-deprecation, too, which is probably why he's about the only guy I know who could get away with this book. Trust me, when he takes a shot, he doesn't miss. It's a good thing he spends just as much time turning his punch-line popgun on himself.

Truth is he's a treasure: a living, breathing catalogue of the laughs and the lighter side of the national obsession, and I'm just the lucky one who got the chance to put these stories on paper, as soon as I stopped laughing.

For my part I would like to thank Cory for being himself, my wife Claire and two sons Ethan and Joe for their enduring love and patience, publishers Warren Adler and Kevin Chapman for taking a punt, Simon White and the team at Rydges Hotel Wellington for the room with a view, and my mum, Jude, for reading the whole thing, and laughing.

Finally, this is for my late father Pete, who taught me to read and encouraged me to write.

Scotty Stevenson
Auckland, 2015

FOREWORD
BY ISRAEL DAGG

I'M ALWAYS HAPPY for my teammates when they tell me they are embarking upon new journeys, but when Cory Jane told me he was writing a book, my only thought was: 'Hell, no!'

Whoever decided to give this man the following 210 pages to tell these stories has some serious explaining to do. Surely, if our honour, our private lives, and our credibility were important to the publishers they would have run a mile, which is exactly what we all did as soon as we found out this book was happening.

I have known Cory for a long time. He has taken years off my life. For the last five years we have roomed together in the All Blacks, which is why these weren't tours for me as much as they were sentences. Speaking of sentences, I'm surprised he could string enough of them together to actually have a book.

What does not surprise me is that he has had a crack at everyone. Cory remembers every damn detail and he will always (should the opportunity present itself) use those details against his teammates. He is a pest — when he finally finishes playing it won't be because he was dropped, it'll be because he was exterminated.

It's our own fault. We all knew this day would come: the day Cory Jane finally spilled the beans on all of us. He can't be trusted, you know. He thinks because he takes a nightly bath that he comes out looking clean. Well, he doesn't. If he thinks he's got dirt on us (and I'll admit, he probably does) then that's nothing compared to what we all have on him.

Oh, yes, we will have our revenge. But, in the meantime, you go ahead and enjoy this book. Just pray, like the rest of us, that there won't be another one.

Izzy Dagg
Christchurch, 2015

1
MORE TARZAN THAN JANE

I WAS BORN in the Wellington suburb of Naenae — or as I like to call it, the suburb so nice they named it twice. I don't know why, but to this day, whenever I meet anyone from Wellington on my travels around the world, they are invariably from Naenae. As a kid, I didn't think the place was that bad, but judging by the number of Naenaeans I have met in other parts of the globe, I'd be bloody surprised if anyone's still living there.

I have one sister, Renee. She is two years older than me and the bully of the family. Growing up under her regime of torture was a nightmare, and I think my growth — physically and mentally — was stunted by her totalitarian rule. I don't think I hit puberty until I was 14 or 15, though there are still a few people who will tell you I haven't quite got there yet.

Renee always used to beat me up. She took seriously my comments about her being the sister I couldn't stand and became instead the big brother I never had. She also took seriously the notion that I was the little sister she had always wanted.

I learnt to be fast and nimble, simply to get away from her. It was a talent that would stand me in good stead later in life. The only real trick I had up my sleeve was that I could always make her laugh. I remember as an eight year old finding Dad's cigarette lighter in his desk drawer and, being too young to consider the consequences, I spent a good half an hour lighting sheets of paper under the desk — just because it looked cool. Unfortunately, I was never great at covering my tracks, and I left all the ashes lying under the desk. I have since discovered that it is a universal law that a boy will never clean up after himself, even when he knows this will get him into trouble.

As it was, I soon tired of trying to burn the house down and I went off to play with my GI Joe (that's not a code name, by the way; I am referring to the actual toy) and didn't think much of it.

Well, I didn't, that is, until Dad got home and hauled Renee and me into the kitchen. We knew we were in for a torrid time, but I had a plan. (I don't have a lot of advice to give, and trust me, you won't find an awful lot of it in this book, but this is something to remember: always sit next to your father when he's angry, and make sure your sibling is facing him directly.)

Renee may have been tougher than me, but she never had a plan.

Dad was midway through the interrogation and my constant and most stringent denials were only serving to wind him up. The pressure was beginning to show on Renee, who knew that with every denial from me, the blame was inching ever closer to her. I seized my opportunity. Just as Dad turned his full attention on Renee, I started pulling my best faces at her. Of course, she couldn't help but laugh. And once she laughed, it was over.

I knew from that moment she was the one who was about to take the fall and I was going free.

I also knew from that moment that getting what you want in life is all about taking opportunities when they are presented.

After that, whatever I could do to blame her, I did. If nothing else, that alone fulfilled me as a child.

Dad was a builder so he would shoot off to work early most days. We had a little dog called Rusty who went everywhere with him. I think Rusty was the kid he wished he'd had. I may have resented that dog a fair bit. Every morning, off Dad would go to work, and every morning Rusty would go with him. I spent many an hour plotting my revenge on that canine interloper.

Mum was a postie, so we spent a fair chunk of our childhood riding in the sorting bin on the front of the mail bike. It would be a sackable offence to carry your kids, *sans* helmets, on your postie bike these days, but

Family on the road. On a getaway with Dad and Renee.

Me posing for the camera, aged five. Hell, I was a cute kid.

things were a little simpler back then.

Often dogs would come tearing out of driveways and Mum would swerve into a wall, or a fence, or a hedge. She was always okay. It was Renee or me who took the punishment. We'd come home with scratches and bruises after each and every run. I think back now and wonder how many times the residents of Upper Hutt went to the mailbox to find power bills and bank statements soaked in the blood of the Jane children.

I even recall once having to stanch the flow of claret from a particularly nasty forearm gash, suffered in a collision with a power pole, on a postcard from the Greek Islands. 'Hi Mum and Dad, Santorini is lovely, but hell it's violent!'

Mum and Dad were hard-working people, and Renee and I were typical hard-playing kids. I may have been a bit more hyper-active than most (and being dad now to a son who actually has ADHD I guess he must have got it from someone) but when Dad has a tool belt and an endless supply of four-by-twos at the ready, and Mum takes you to work on the front of a two-wheeled death trap, you can't help but get a little bit tough.

I didn't get in a lot of trouble as a kid, but there was always potential.

Unlike now it was standard practice for five and six year olds to have a certain amount of roaming freedom in our neighbourhood. Maybe the community was stronger back then, maybe the freedom we enjoyed was just an illusion, and even when we thought no one was watching us, someone actually was. Regardless, there was always someone to make mischief with and my cousin Kurt and I certainly made our fair share.

Our favourite game was to throw stones at people's houses until the owner came to the window to figure out what was going on. As soon as we saw the curtains shift we'd tear around the other side of their house and start all over again. It must have driven them insane.

We soon tired of throwing stones and upgraded to throwing lemons. We also upgraded from houses to moving cars. I've always prided myself on good hand–eye coordination and maybe that was when I first started to hone the skill. We would see the cars coming through the gap between the houses on the corner, and time our throw so as they drove past the end of our street they were hammered with a barrage of citrus. I'm amazed we didn't cause a pile up.

I was a naughty kid, but loveable, really. I was a cute kid, too, until I was at school. Then I was ugly. I think a lot of that had to do with Mum dressing me.

Later in my school life I also made the mistake of using Dad's Brylcreem and wearing his Brut 33 aftershave. I laid a great burley trail down the school corridors, but I didn't lay much else.

I was a hyper little kid but, fortunately, I loved anything that involved running, catching, kicking, hitting or throwing. I was five when I first ventured into the world of organised sport. My sister played in a T-ball team and

Aged three on the police bike. I think I had stolen it from the neighbour's place!

one day they were a player short. I stepped in, with my parents' blessing (if not my sister's) and started cracking hits all over the park. I thought it was the best thing ever, but then Renee must have got jealous so she started teasing me. What I hadn't realised at the time was that it was an all-girl team. And I was the only fella.

Renee's taunting continued without pause. It got so intense that when we arrived for the big tournament of the year, I refused to step out of the van. The coaches begged and pleaded but the damage was done; I was traumatised. Still it brought new meaning to the phrase 'You're the man'. Even if it's not quite the same when it's

A typical primary school shot. It says Standard 2–3, but I was probably the only Standard 3 kid. I'm in the middle row, fourth from left.

used in a literal sense. I was, after all, the only man.

I was so typical of Kiwi kids. If it involved running around and acting crazy, I was into it. Soon enough I found my way into rugby, not that I really had any choice.

We moved to Upper Hutt when I was six. Upper Hutt gets a bad rap and I have no idea why. The people are great, the haircuts wonderful, and the full facial tattoos are optional. Upper Hutt is still my home and it's a great town, and the sister city to Mesa, Arizona, home of the amazingly named Olympic swimming champion, Misty Hyman. Mesa's population is 81 per cent white, but Upper Hutt still boasts the most bogans per capita.

I attended the local primary schools growing up. I don't know why, but in the suburbs it seems every primary school is named after the street it's on. The two I attended were Rata Street School and Fraser Crescent

The bully of the family. Renee makes me look like a midget as we head off to school. She was in third form and I was in the first form.

School (which for some reason we all called Fraser Street School). We wanted to feel like the flash kids so we put the Street first. I don't know if there is a Saint Rata or a Saint Fraser but it made us feel better about things!

I survived primary school and made my way to Heretaunga College. To be honest I was only there for rugby.

I just did not get school one bit. I was on the back foot from the moment I walked through the college gates, anyway — Renee had gone there ahead of me and needless to say she had created a pretty choice reputation for all Janes to follow. 'Are you Renee's brother?' the teachers would ask. As soon as I said 'yes' I would instantly regret it. And they would, too.

Despite not wanting to be there, I made a deal with

myself to at least turn up. I don't think I ever passed a subject but at least I could say I had a good attendance record! Seriously, though, I just didn't get it. Teachers would write things on the board and I'd stare at their scribblings without understanding a single thing. It could have been Egyptian hieroglyphics for all I knew.

As for maths, well, I don't mind when it's just adding numbers together, but suddenly when everyone was trying to find the value of *x* and *a* and *b* I was done for. Pi was something I had for lunch.

You often had to get up and read extracts in front of the class and I would always put it in my own language. We'd be reading *Lord of the Flies* and I'd be up front 'reading' and it would always come out something like 'So, you know, there was these fullas, and they got stranded on an island, and then they all got spears and stuff and you know got straight up gangster on each other . . .'

The teacher was never impressed.

It got to the point where I didn't even take a bag to school. I turned up knowing I would be getting detention for something (it didn't matter if I hadn't actually done anything, I always got the rap, and I soon discovered that the face-pulling trick only worked at home) and that was about it for the school day. The school bell would ring, I would get detention. The school bell would ring again, I would go home.

That was pretty much my school days. I was put in all the remedial classes because I was deemed to be not smart enough. I think I was the only English-speaking kid ever to be put into the 'English as a Second Language' class.

I didn't much enjoy that, so I would walk around to the gym and find the nearest PE class and ask the other students who wasn't there that day. When that kid's name was read out in roll call I'd call out 'Present' from the back. It was amazing how often this worked, even when I was a seventh former, and the class was for third formers. I may have set the record for the most PE classes attended in a single school year.

The only other thing about school that fulfilled me was hustling other kids outside the tuck shop. My mate Sebastian and I would beg our way through the recess in 10 and 20 cent increments. You would be amazed at how this adds up over the course of a lunchtime. And, better still, at the end of lunch everything was available at reduced prices. It was a great scheme.

We didn't consider ourselves to be beggars. We liked to think of ourselves as salesmen — and what we were selling was our own pitiful circumstances.

We also truly believed that this was the best kind of accounting class, as we would always be constantly calculating how much we needed for a cream bun, and how much we had.

The only bad thing was that everyone started to avoid us. That wasn't the kind of reputation we were after. Even today, when I walk through the Upper Hutt shops, someone will stop to remind me that I owe them $2.80.

Apart from endless PE and relieving other students of their coins, I just didn't want to be there. There are three things that I hated doing then, and still hate to this day: standing up in front of people to talk, and writing on a whiteboard for others to read.

I write like a three year old. My kids are always asking me to write something for them, but they have neater handwriting than me.

The final thing is trying to spell something. See, this is the problem with school: I would ask a teacher how to spell, for instance, 'hippopotamus', to which she would invariably reply, 'Look it up in the dictionary, Cory.' My response was always the same. 'Miss, if I don't know how to spell it, how the hell am I going to find it in a dictionary!'

Somehow I managed to get all the way through to the final year of high school, though how much of what I had been taught had managed to find a permanent home in my brain is debatable. Eventually, the teachers must have lost patience because one day I was corralled into a room where I was told that I may as well leave school. I didn't consider it an expulsion as such; it seemed far too polite for that.

I went home that night and told Mum and Dad, and decided to see the week out at least. The following day I got home and Mum looked a tad concerned. 'Your dad had a few drinks last night and went to see the principal,' she told me. I feared the worst. What on earth would he have said, I wondered. Turns out he had called them fulltime babysitters, and terrible ones at that. Suffice to

My wife think's I'm still mummy's boy and she's probably right! Here I am aged 12. I think mum dressed me for this one.

say, the principal didn't change his mind, and my school days were officially over.

Let's be honest, they all knew I would rather be doing something else anyway so they were just expediting the process.

I wasn't a nasty kid — I never swore at teachers or spent lunchtimes tagging the bike sheds — I just had zero application. I would often be asked to leave class during the day, which I thought was great because I could then go and kick a rugby ball around.

Every teacher had asked me what I wanted to be when I left school and, from the age of six, I had the same answer: I wanted to be an All Black. Actually, that's not exactly true. I didn't *want* to be an All Black, I knew I was *going to be* an All Black.

That sounds cocky, and maybe it was, but from the age of six I had told anyone who cared to listen, 'I am going to be an All Black.'

2
FALLING FOR THE GAME

I WAS ONLY FIVE YEARS OLD when Dad, who was always keen to find ways to tire me out, suggested I give rugby a go. I can't remember if he was wielding a piece of four by two at the time, but regardless of whether it was a suggestion or straight coercion, I went along and played my first game for the under-six team at the Rimutaka club with my neighbour Steven. He lasted all of half the first game until he got stood on, and then he was done. I don't know what happened to Steven, but I'm picking he never went into the shoe business.

While Steven's brief rugby career lasted all of 20 minutes, I couldn't get enough of it. I scored two tries that day, and loved every second being out there with the ball and the boys on the grass of Maoribank Park. And that's where I stayed and played, at the Rimutaka club, until

Trophy time. Cleaning up in junior rugby with Rimutaka. I may not have passed the ball, but I scored all the tries!

I was 12 years old. I'm not entirely sure my teammates were ever grateful for that loyalty.

I don't think I was a bad teammate. I got along with everyone, was 'back of the year' every year, and always played my hardest. But the fact I played first-five and NEVER passed the ball may have led to some simmering resentment among the rest of the boys.

I scored 55 tries one year. Which I thought was pretty good but, again, it was only because I never passed the ball.

As soon as I had the ball in my hands I just tried to step my way through the opposing team. People ask, 'Where did you learn this or that?' The simple answer, and the truth, is that I don't know. Learning has never been a forte of mine! I just played rugby. I knew I couldn't bump people off — I got beaten up by my sister, remember? — so I guess in some ways it was survival instinct. I was a tiny kid, and avoiding people seemed the best way to avoid being hurt.

Dad coached me for one year and, gee, he was mean. He made a couple of kids cry, but mainly he took it out on me.

If anything went wrong he'd turn to me and bark, 'Cory, get off the field and go sit down.' It was always my fault. He may have been tough, but he has always been a big supporter of mine and while he is a massive footy fan he has never taken any credit for any of my talents. This actually led me to believe (a belief I held for some years as a child) that I was adopted.

Despite working long hours, Dad would always find a way to make time to come outside and kick a ball with me and, when he wasn't around, I designed my own practice field for goal-kicking out the front of my house. The goalposts were imaginary and consisted of uprights contrived from the chimney and the hip of the roof, with the guttering acting as the crossbar. It was almost perfect, apart from one major flaw: the lounge room window.

I cannot tell you how many times a potential game-winning kick went through that window, and it's probably no surprise that I haven't been handed the tee much in my professional career. Dad would explode every time he heard the glass shattering, but the anger would soon subside; I think he could deal with the glazier being on speed dial if it meant I was trying to get better.

After rugby season came cricket season. That window never stood a chance.

I would have found another spot to practice but our house was surrounded on two sides by toetoe bushes, which Kiwis will know by the more common name, 'cutty grass'. If a ball went into the toetoe, that's where it stayed, and not because I was afraid of the sharp leaves, but because I was petrified of spiders.

I am still petrified of spiders. Piri Weepu once picked up a dead spider in the Hurricanes gym and I set all kinds of franchise speed records getting myself the hell out of there. I have always liked a prank on the boys, and have never minded being the target of one myself, but if there are arachnids involved, you'd better be prepared to put your dukes up, because I'll be throwing them!

Jimmy 'Donger' Cowan found this out the hard way on a tour to South Africa in 2010. Jimmy had become an easy mark for our wee trio of tricksters, which comprised Israel Dagg, Zac Guildford and me.

It wasn't that we had anything against Jimmy, it was more a case that we knew he wasn't smart enough to get us back.

Jimmy had spent the afternoon taunting me about my arachnophobia so we planned a pre-emptive strike. We asked our South African security guard if we could borrow his Taser and, like all good, responsible security guards he asked us what we wanted it for. When we told him we just wanted to scare Jimmy, he immediately handed it over to us. Looking back, I'm not sure that was

Jimmy 'Donger' Cowan obviously upset after our pre-emptive strike in South Africa. He's taking the ball and he's going home . . .

the most responsible thing for a security guard to do.

Once we had the Taser our next stop was reception, where we asked for a key to Jimmy's room. The receptionist duly obliged (again, I'm not entirely sure that was the most responsible thing to be doing). To protect ourselves we also told the receptionist that if anyone came looking for a key to our rooms they would require a special word. I think we chose 'Mataura', Jimmy's home town, just to make the whole thing feel right. Mataura's a great place: famous for one river, one freezing works, and two idiot halfbacks.

The timing couldn't have been better. We let ourselves into Jimmy's room just as he was getting out of the shower and with Taser bared we went for him. We taped up his feet and taped his arms around him before we signed his forehead and left him there.

We stood outside for a good 20 minutes, where we could hear him struggling, and failing, to free himself. It was only when the crying stopped that we thought we had better set him loose.

Jimmy latched onto Ali Williams for moral support and together they immediately set about hatching a plan for vengeance. Ali loved a practical joke and his one supreme talent was that he was always prepared to take things further than anyone else. That night he sidled up beside me at dinner and gently whispered in my ear, 'I have seen your future, CJ. And it involves very big spiders.'

'Ali,' I said, 'I would punch my own sister if she came at

me with a spider, so I'm just warning you, I will be coming out swinging.' I think it was the first and last time anyone in the All Blacks has ever taken me seriously!

I had quickly become a rugby tragic as a kid, and I remember as an eight year old rushing home from school in the middle of the week to write down (poorly) all the division one fixtures for the weekend. Then I would get my boots and my ball and head off to the park. If Canterbury, for instance, was facing Otago, I knew Andrew Mehrtens was playing so I would force myself to kick goals like Andrew Mehrtens. If Tony Brown was the other first-five, I tried to kick goals like Tony Brown. If I knew a player kicked with his left foot, then so did I.

I never really had heroes as such, or guys I wanted to copy wholesale. I watched EVERYONE, and practised the things they did. I might have liked a particular kick a player put in, or a fend, or a step, or an angle he might have entered the backline. It was pick and mix rugby. My dad was always prodding me to improve my skills. He would say, 'You're playing first-five so you need to kick with both feet.' So I would watch left-footed kickers and practise what they did.

My team was Wellington, of course, but Dad was from Wairoa (*Top Town* champions, 1990) in Hawke's Bay.

He was a dyed-in-the-wool Magpies fan so I grew up watching guys like the late Jarrod Cunningham, Gordon Falcon, Murdoch Paewai and others. Dad was so excited when Hawke's Bay made the division two final against

Southland in 1994 that we booked a date on the couch to watch it. Unfortunately, I forgot, and spent the afternoon at a mate's place.

Southland won the match 20–18, and Dad didn't talk to me for a week. Full forgiveness would only come a decade later when I spent a season playing for the Magpies. Let this be a lesson to you: never underestimate a man's passion for his provincial rugby team. Dad has still never forgiven Norm Hewitt for leaving Hawke's Bay to play for Southland in 1995. That's a grudge that has lasted for 20 years . . . and counting!

Dad may have growled at me a few times as a coach, but I don't remember too many of those tellings off because more often than not I was probably already knocked out. And here's why: I could not tackle.

Seriously, for me, making a tackle meant trying to get any part of my body in the way. Unfortunately it was usually my head.

It's a good thing we take concussion more seriously these days, but in those days you'd be out cold in the first game and then playing in the next. Come to think of it, maybe that's why I spent my school life in remedial classes.

Concussion is a major concern these days, and while you can't prevent head clashes in a contact sport like rugby, you can at least make sure every care is taken after a player has suffered a knock.

I was KO'd in a Super Rugby match against the Stormers in 2010 when I was run over by giant Fijian winger Sireli

Stormers winger Sireli Naqelevuki has just run over me on the way to scoring against the 'Canes. I was out for the count.

Naqelevuki. In fairness, he had about 40 kilograms on me, but I knew that my only chance of stopping him close to the line was to go after the ball. Big mistake. I missed the ball and got his head and shoulder instead. I hit the deck face first, and all reports say I was lying there breathing like a tranquillised bull. I came to in the doctor's room under the stand and went through my testing.

'Are you okay, my friend?' the doctor was asking.

'Yep, good as gold,' I replied.

'So do you remember who you played last week?'

I couldn't remember a thing. And sure enough I was

told that I would not be returning to play. I think the diagnosis was given more credence by the fact I got off the table and started scrubbing up as if I was waiting to perform surgery, and then I started speaking with a South African accent.

I was in a lot of pain after that match and the team doctor decided that he would room with me to keep an eye on me. I wasn't allowed to go to sleep so the light was on which was making me feel even worse. The doctor asked if I was hungry. 'No, Doc, I feel pretty nauseous actually,' I told him. So then he ordered food for himself!

Here I am, head pounding, light hurting my eyes, stomach churning, and the bloody doctor is munching on a burger.

If that wasn't bad enough, there came a knock at the door and Piri Weepu appeared. Piri told the doctor that he would take over, so the doctor told him to set an alarm and make sure that he checked on me at regular intervals. Piri gave him assurances that he would stay up all night. Next thing I know the alarm is going and bloody Piri is snoring his head off.

'Piri!' I yelled. 'I could have bloody died!' 'But you didn't CJ,' he replied, 'and that's the main thing.' Then he rolled over and went back to sleep.

Despite having a terrible tackling technique as a child, I still loved every minute out there playing. Every year I felt like I was getting better at the game, but there was just one problem: I was a scrawny weed of a kid and I never seemed to get any bigger.

After making the Hutt Valley under-12 team as a fullback, representative rugby always seemed like something I was not destined to experience again. Things had got a fair bit harder when I was intermediate age — it seemed all the kids were bigger than me. When I went on to Heretaunga College I played in the under-55 kg class, but could have played under-45 kg, if they'd had a team. By 15 I was brave enough to trial for the first XV but I was that tiny the only position I could handle was halfback. I didn't make the first XV so played halfback for the seconds. There was only one problem: I never passed the ball.

I did manage to get a trial for the Wellington under-16 team as a halfback. I ended up missing out on that, too. And the next year, I missed out again. It was a frustrating period for me.

How was I going to be an All Black if I couldn't even make the Wellington under-16 team? Even Ma'a Nonu made that team and, really, he didn't amount to much!

I still think about that period of my rugby life and it still frustrates me that I never got a crack. Even all these years later, having achieved so many of my goals in sport, I feel like I was punished in a way for not being at one of the bigger schools. I think it is even harder now for a kid to be noticed if he or she is playing for a school that is not considered to be a rugby powerhouse. Heretaunga

College was a second division team and I naively thought that it shouldn't matter what school or division you played in; if you were good enough you would make it.

In my final year at Heretaunga we had a great season and played Mana College in the final. The first-five for Mana was a bloke called Tamati Ellison and I was marking him. Unfortunately earlier in the year we'd had a school trip to Australia and the boys decided it would be a good idea to shave our heads. Eventually I buckled under the pressure, and had mine shaved, too. So then I had the worst-looking bald head in the world.

Even SANZAR CEO Greg Peters (left) had a better-looking head than me, and his looks like a half-cracked emu egg. My looks went straight from Brad Pitt to Bruce Willis.

If that wasn't bad enough, we also decided to dye the regrowth blond. The Heretaunga College team that took the field that day looked like 15 Eminems. And I was the most Slim Shady of the lot.

People ask me today why I always wear track pants on the training field (and trust me, if I could play in them, too, I would) and I can probably trace the answer back to that college final. It was bad enough that I had a peroxided kiwifruit head, but given my self-esteem was already at an all-time low, I also realised that day that there was something else dramatically wrong with me: I had two pipe cleaners for legs; two horrible skinny pins sticking out the bottom of my shorts.

You can picture that final now: here's me, the skinny Eminem clone with the toothpicks sticking out of his short shorts and there's Tamati Ellison, descendant of the great Tom Ellison, with his head of luscious hair and his big Maori thighs! We still won that day, but it was Tamati who got noticed.

I wore a beanie for six whole months after that, even on the hottest days in summer. And I pray that I don't go bald later in life, like Israel Dagg (right).

With school behind me, I had to find a job, and with very little in the way of formal education to fall back on, I found myself making timber pallets. I was happy that someone had offered me paid employment to be honest, but balancing real world responsibilities with rugby aspirations wasn't easy.

I made the Wellington Rugby Academy programme as an 18 year old, but I had to pay the bills and couldn't go to training all day. For the first couple of years I would get up at five in the morning, drive into Wellington, train in the morning, drive back to Upper Hutt, work my job at Carters, finish work, drive back into Wellington to train in the evening and then drive back to Upper Hutt. After

My first game for the Upper Hutt Premiers, 2002. Getting my fend working against Avalon.

A pre-season appearance for the Wellington XV against Hawke's Bay at my home ground, Maidstone Park. Luke Mahoney is in support and Christian Cullen is tracking the play.

a couple of years of that I thought, I can't keep doing this!

I had come to the realisation that if I didn't start taking things seriously, I was never going to live up to the promises I had made as a six-year-old boy. Remember, I didn't *want* to be an All Black, I knew I was *going to be* an All Black. A bunch of us had moved to the Stokes Valley Club to play colts. We won the competition and a year later I moved back to Upper Hutt and began playing premier club rugby. I made the Wellington colts that year and at the back end of that season, in 2003, I made the Wellington Lions squad.

I also made the New Zealand under-21 trials, but the fullbacks were Glen Horton and Ben Atiga who had both already played Super Rugby so they didn't have to trial.

When the team was announced I wasn't in it, but I was asked to head north with them as a training partner. I was either good enough to be in the team or I wasn't, I thought to myself. There was no way I was going all that way to hold tackle bags.

Maybe I was impatient, or maybe I didn't have the right attitude, or maybe it was a mix of both, but whatever the reason, after just two appearances for the Lions in the 2003 season — against Otago and Northland — coaches Chris Boyd and John Plumtree gave me an ultimatum for the 2004 season: I could play for Wellington B or I could head north to Hawke's Bay on loan.

I chose to go, and I was not surprised I was loaned out. I mean, I would turn up to Wellington fitness testing in my sneakers and three-quarter pants. You should never turn up to anything in three-quarter pants.

So began my first and last experience of playing for another province, and I didn't do it alone. Cory Aporo came with me, as did my future wife Amie. We treated it as a bit of an adventure and, because we were on loan from Wellington, we were put up in a hotel complex in Napier. Unfortunately it was a one-bedroom unit, and you don't have to be the brightest person in the world to figure out that meant that while Amie and I had the bedroom, not far away Cory Aporo slept on the couch.

Fijian sevens player Nasoni Rokobiau also stayed in the hotel complex, but he had a two-bedroom apartment. Every week we would ask him if he would swap with us, but every week he would tell us that his wife and kids were coming to stay.

I don't know if he was just lying because he quite enjoyed having all that room to himself, but I can tell you this: no wife or kids ever came, and Aporo spent that whole season on the couch, blocking his ears.

It was good to go away and grow up a bit. At least I think I grew up a bit.

Kieran Keane, or KK as everyone knows him, was the coach at that stage, and that man could fire up like none before him. This is the guy who once, as a teacher, got so upset with a kid in his class that he told him to go out into the carpark and count the stones. An hour later the kid came back and gave him a number. KK just looked at

Kieran Keane, who could fire up like none before him.

him and said, 'Wrong! Go and try again.' There is also the tale of a particularly dumb prop under his watch who was having so much trouble figuring out a lineout move that KK told him to go count the needles on the pine tree at the end of the field. Rumour has it, the prop is still there, wishing he had more fingers and toes!

KK had a way with words and pretty much everyone in the team was called 'mutton head'.

He was a tough coach and he expected us to give it our all. I had missed a game against East Coast with a sore ankle and he called Cory Aporo and me into the office for a chat. Once we were seated, he began pouring praise on Aporo, telling him how good it was to see him making such an effort.

I was thinking I was in for a pretty good pep talk as well after that, but the smile drained away from his face as he turned to me and shouted, 'As for you. Well, you can lift your game!' And then we were dismissed. I was shocked. I was the top try-scorer in the bloody team!

I guess he knew that I thought the whole thing was a bit of a laugh and he was desperate for me to take the game seriously. I think about that once in a while — he must have seen so many kids like me in his time as a teacher and as a coach.

You should always be thankful when a coach takes the time to make you work harder. It shows they care.

Scoring for Hawke's Bay in the 2004 NPC second division final against Nelson Bays. Sadly, the mutton heads lost.

It was a great crew up there in Hawke's Bay and we had a lot of fun. KK knew how to get the best out of people and even then you could tell he had great ideas as a coach. We had one move he called 'the hinge', but none of us could figure it out so we called it 'the door'. This drove him crazy: 'For God's sake why is this so hard? You mutton heads!'

We lost to Nelson Bays in the final. That hurt KK plenty. I shouldn't have been surprised, though. I have still never won an NPC or ITM Championship, despite making plenty of finals. When I made that first one with Hawke's Bay I thought that was going to be the start of something great. Turns out it was the start of something long and tough.

3
GOING SEVENS & GOING SUPER

THE 2005 SEASON was a disappointing one for me. While my exile to Hawke's Bay was over, I played in just two matches for the Lions before being out for all but the last couple of matches of the season. Something, though, had caught my attention earlier that year, and that was watching Tamati Ellison, my old Mana College nemesis, playing sevens for New Zealand at Westpac Stadium.

I made a mental note: you have got to get amongst that! At the end of the 2005 season I was picked up in the Hurricanes wider training group but was asked if I wanted to go down to Queenstown at the beginning of 2006 to play for the Wellington Sevens side. At 23 years old, with my long hair and my Alice headband and my skinny legs, I headed to the national tournament for a taste of what I had seen in Wellington the year before.

Nothing compares to Titch's sevens training regime.

I was by no means the youngest guy in the team. He was just 15 years old. His name was Julian Savea.

I made Gordon Tietjens' training camp after the tournament, and immediately wished I hadn't. 'Titch' tells everyone the same thing when they arrive at camp, and it goes like this: 'You'll never work harder than you do in this camp, so give your all.' I took him at his word and gave him my all, and it was sure enough the hardest I have ever worked in my life.

When camp came to a close I was told I had made the national team. I was rapt to have been selected and couldn't wait to get back to Wellington to train with the Hurricanes. There was only one problem: when I arrived at Rugby League Park the next day, I couldn't walk.

Without a word of a lie, Hurricanes coach Colin Cooper was standing there looking at me and I literally couldn't get out of my car. It must have taken a good 20 minutes to extract myself from the driver's seat and when I finally did get out and made my way onto the field, I couldn't run. Coops, who I am sure was doing his best not to laugh, wandered over.

'What's the matter with you, CJ?' he asked.

'Um, to be honest with you Coops, I can't really move.'

I felt like a complete idiot, but the medical staff took pity on me and sent me home to ice up. For two whole days! It's hard to believe someone thought it was a good idea to give Titch a knighthood.

Gordon Tietjens receives his knighthood from Governor-General Sir Jerry Mateparae in 2013.

What was he knighted for? Services to athlete cruelty? No wonder Super Rugby coaches don't want him to have their players.

I have been in a lot of training sessions but nothing has ever compared to the sevens regime. On that first camp we were subjected to a phosphate test, which is designed to record your ability to repeat performance over a series of 40-metre sprints with a small rest in between. After that we were subjected to a beep test which is designed to test your aerobic capacity. Once you had run yourself into the ground, the skill sessions begin.

Titch's trainings are designed to break you. Former New Zealand sevens player Hayden Reid worked himself so hard in one of Titch's testing sessions that he was admitted to Tauranga Hospital and put on a drip. Better still, later that day Titch came into the ward to see him, and started *laughing* at him. Best of all, he turned to the poor guy and said, 'Reido, do you think you could get out of here this afternoon because I still need to see you play before I can pick you.'

Typical Titch: hospitalising yourself is still not good enough to make his team.

Everything Titch puts you through in a training session is designed to find out how much you are prepared to give. In his eyes, you just need to give 100 per cent. If you've only got 50 per cent left to give, he'll demand you give 100 per cent of that 50 per cent. If you have 20 per cent left to give, you need to give 100 per cent of that. Actually, that's probably half the problem: all that talk about percentages had me lost after the first 10 minutes.

Being a part of the sevens team taught me to go hard, and to never give up. There is so much space in the game that you have to learn how to take care of business. In fifteens you have plenty of guys on the field who can cover you if you make a mistake. In sevens, one mistake and you cost your team points. It's no surprise to me that so many of Titch's guys go on to be stars in the test arena, too — under him you develop exceptional skills and become accustomed to pressure, to big stadiums, and to the tournament atmosphere.

The 2006 season was Commonwealth Games year, but we had been terrible to start the season. We had not advanced from the Cup semi-finals in either of the first

Trying to hold up Fiji's Epeli Dranivasa in the semi-final of the 2006 LA Sevens tournament. We lost narrowly.

two tournaments of the year and it was fair to say there was a bit of frustration within the team.

After we played the Los Angeles tournament, which was the second event after Wellington, we decided to let our hair down with a couple of beers. Needless to say, we didn't exactly have Titch's approval. I'd had a fair few over the course of the evening and suddenly I desperately wanted to get back to the hotel. I could actually see it from where we were and figured it wouldn't take long to walk to.

Now, it's one thing to grow up in Upper Hutt where no one had fences and where you spent your adolescence scuttling through people's backyards to get away from the car you just hit with a lemon, but it's quite another thing to start taking short cuts to your team hotel through the back yards of Californians. How I didn't get shot is a miracle.

I was about half a dozen fences into my epic journey, and by now completely disorientated, when I jumped over a gate and straight into a police officer.

A Los Angeles policeman is a trigger happy type at the best of times, so God knows how close he'd come to firing when out of the blue came a half drunk Kiwi rugby player.

'Come here, son,' he said.

I turned around and looked at him, swaying all the while.

'Nah, I'm cool, I'm just going over there,' I said, pointing to the hotel, which, incredibly I had somehow managed to find.

'Son, come here,' he repeated a little more sternly.

I thought better of bolting, and after a small but to-the-point conversation he told me to haul ass back to the hotel and go straight to bed!

I thought that was good advice, but I couldn't remember what room I was in. I was busy trying my key in every door I could find when Dwayne Sweeney popped his head out of his room and told me to get inside. I did as I was told and jumped straight into bed, just like I had been told to by the policeman. Poor old Sweens must have had a pretty uncomfortable night on the couch.

When I came to in the morning, I had no idea whose room I was in. I was in a pair of undies and nothing else and in my haste to gather my thoughts and get back to my own digs I walked straight out of the room and right into the entire team — coaches and all — who were lined up down the hallway waiting for me. No one was very impressed.

It dawned on me on the flight back to New Zealand that we were all trying to make the Commonwealth Games team. We all knew the stories of guys training themselves to a standstill and missing out on the final cut. It was going to be a hard enough job to make that team as it was, without any extramural activities.

When Titch rang me to tell me I had made the Games squad, I let him know how sorry I was for letting the team down in Los Angeles. Fortunately it was at the end of a tournament, which meant the team didn't have to pay for my sins.

That was the other thing about Gordon Tietjens: he was an equal opportunity torturer. No one ever had to take a punishment on their own because everyone had to do it with them. If he caught a guy eating the skin on the chicken, we would all be on the line the next day. If you didn't make your '80-60-40s' in time, you got another, and another, and another . . .

And it didn't even have to be us making the mistakes. Julian Savea and I were talking about sevens one day and he was shaking his head about the team having to do extras because of something out of their control.

Titch is a massive tennis fan. So much so that when he was a kid in Rotorua he pretended to be Maori just so he could play in a Maori tennis tournament. He reckoned no one would be able to tell he was Pakeha, but if you've seen him you'd know he's the palest Maori since Christian Cullen.

Anyway, he's also a massive Roger Federer fan, and Julian said the boys would pray that the Fed Express would win his matches because if he lost, Titch would take it out on the team. I don't know too many coaches who get emotional over Swiss tennis stars but, then again, Sir Gordon Tietjens ain't like other coaches.

Despite knowing full well that if I got caught I would be on the line, I always had goodies in my room — I love my fizzies and my lollies so I ran a clandestine tuck shop on tour. I was like Morgan Freeman in *The Shawshank Redemption* — the guy in prison who knows how to get things from time to time. I'm glad I never got caught because there is no way I would have been able to handle sevens without my sugar hits.

I also couldn't go without pulling the occasional prank on the boys, and I had a willing accomplice in Tafai Ioasa. Eric Rush always used to tell everyone that he thought Tafai ran onto the field with sunglasses on, but then he realised they were his nostrils.

Ahead of the Hong Kong tournament that year Tafai and I turned the whole team floor upside down: we flipped beds, hid laptops, stashed wallets — if it wasn't tied or bolted down it was flipped.

Once the deed was complete, we headed off to town, only to return to find the team at DEFCON 1. Lote Raikabula was more worried than most, and was jumping about the place claiming his wallet had been stolen. For most of us that was the first time we actually knew Lote had a wallet because we had never seen it come out before.

Lote was so distraught that a team meeting was called by the manager Ross Everiss. He sat us all down and demanded a confession.

Of course, I was still thinking back to my LA hijinks so I wasn't in the mood to come forward. Eventually Rossco told us that he was going to have to call the police, at which point Tafai and I finally broke.

Now, this is where things get strange: eat a bit of chicken skin, and you get sprints all day. Have a couple of beers after a tournament and you get the silent treatment. But trash the entire team's rooms and almost cause a diplomatic incident and you get congratulated for pulling off a great prank.

Tafai and I were thinking about what we were going to say to Titch and there he is laughing his ass off while the boys are throwing death stares at us. Titch then proceeded to tell me about how he liked putting live goats in his teammates' rooms, amongst other stories of the pranks of yore. I left him giggling to himself about rooms filled with goat shit and wandered off to make sure my room hadn't been touched in a revenge attack.

Every New Zealand sevens player will tell you the same thing about their experience in the side: it is one of the most close-knit teams in rugby, on the field and off it, and

Scoring against England in the gold medal match at the 2006 Commonwealth Games in Melbourne.

you have to find ways to have fun to make up for the pain of playing . . . and, of course, Roger Federer's occasional dips in form.

We rolled into the Commonwealth Games knowing there was real pressure on us to make it three straight gold medals, and the tournament went well. We ended up defeating England 29–21 in the final to keep New Zealand's perfect record at the Games intact. It was our first tournament win of the season and it meant plenty to the boys, and to Titch, too.

The Commonwealth Games gold medal meant everything to the team. We gave it plenty after the final.

GOING SEVENS & GOING SUPER

The big hair and the Alice band turned me into an overnight sex symbol.

That year, 2006, was also the year of the Alice band. Now I know what you're going to say here, and before you do, let me remind you, it was 2006 and I *was* a sex symbol. Things could have been worse, I could have been rolling a man bun.

But here's the truth — I wanted dreads and so while I was growing my hair I had to keep it out of my eyes. Now I love Nick 'The Honey Badger' Cummins' strict adherence to the traditional head tape, but nothing says comfortable like a loop of elastic. If I was going to cement my place in the Hurricanes I knew I had to fit in and so when I turned up to pre-season my hair was dreaded and I was ready to roll.

No sooner had I walked into the training base than Ma'a Nonu told me to cut them off. He was convinced I was copying his style. Considering we also had Rodney So'oialo and Tana Umaga with dreads in the team, I'm not entirely sure how he thought it was *his* style I was copying, but there was no point in arguing.

The way I looked at it, they were all big 'Moans and I was bringing some real style to proceedings. I think, ultimately, they were just intimidated by the blond streaking, and by the fact I made the dreads look half decent.

Ma'a was unmoved. He told me that unless I cut them off I would get a beating every day at training. Now this is not a fair fight; Ma'a is twice my size and his temper is twice as quick. I put it to him that I would have to

Me and my dreads . . . they didn't meet with universal approval.

enlist some help, but it was no use: the three dreadlocked Samoans were in it together. There wasn't anyone in the team that was willing to help me take them on! It was like a Samoan hydra — if you went after one of them, two would come back!

I had no choice, really. The dreadlocks lasted just a few months and, for a while, I thought that was about as long as my Super Rugby career was going to last as well.

That's because I got my first telling off from Tana Umaga in South Africa on my very first tour. We had played against the Sharks in Durban and half the team went out for a couple of drinks while the rest of us stayed behind. I was rooming with Conrad Smith and both of us had recovery in the morning so we had hit the sack early. When the morning came, I opened my eyes to see 'Snakey' leaving the room. In my half asleep state I didn't think too

The Samoan hydra . . . . Rodney, Tana and Ma'a.

In action against the Sharks in 2007. I was in trouble the next morning.

hard about it and closed my eyes again. Then there was a knock on the door followed by a voice telling me to get my ass down to recovery!

Now, any decent roommate would have woken me up, but not Conrad Smith. He's so selfish.

I reckon he must have taken one look at me and thought, 'This guy's got potential to move to centre so I may as well ruin him now.' Everyone bangs on about his legal qualifications, but well before law school he had a degree in looking out for number one!

By the time I got down to recovery there were just three people in the room: Alby Mathewson, Blair Stewart and David Smith. They were all battling serious hangovers, while I had simply slept it. Not that it mattered. To anyone looking on it would have seemed that I had been out on the diesel as well.

Then Tana walked into the room, and if you know Tana you know how good he is to talk to about things. He's a really softly spoken guy who always has time for a word with the young guys. This wasn't going to be too bad at all! I was thinking about the way he had welcomed me into the team at the beginning of the year and the supportive words he'd had with me during the season. I was thinking about this when he walked straight up to me, and began to speak.

'Who the hell do you think you are?' he thundered at me. Okay, it *was* going to be bad. 'You think you can come into this team and just do what you bloody want?' He continued. We were speechless. And if the introductory questions were tough, the next 10 minutes were even tougher. We all learnt a valuable lesson that day: don't mess with Tana.

Tana made it clear that we were the dogsbodies for the next week, which wouldn't have been so bad except for the fact that the other guys were being sent home to prepare for the first game back in New Zealand while I was the only one staying on to play the last game of the tour. I'd be taking the punishment all on my own.

I hate cleaning things up so you can imagine how much I enjoyed my punishment. All week I was loading training gear, unloading training gear, cleaning up the sheds, and being bossed around by the senior players.

Then I had to clean everyone's boots before we left South Africa. You have no idea how demeaning and embarrassing that was.

I was beginning to think that my rugby career would be forever defined by self-sabotage and an uncanny ability to get myself into trouble: the lack of effort at the Lions which had seen me loaned to Hawke's Bay, the drinking session in LA which could have cost me a place at the Commonwealth Games, and now a basic failure in following procedure with the Hurricanes . . . what was it with me?

I made the decision to work harder than ever, and that year I went on to become the only Hurricanes back to play in every game of the season. If I could just keep the momentum, my All Blacks dream could be closer than I thought. That turned out to be one of the best decisions I have made.

4
FULFILLING A PROMISE

I FELT GOOD heading into the 2008 Super Rugby season and again I managed to keep myself fit, playing 12 of the 14 games that year, which ended for us in a losing effort in the semi-final against the Crusaders. I knew my form was good, but I wasn't quite there yet. I hunkered down for the Air New Zealand Cup season with the Lions, knowing I just had to keep improving if I wanted my shot.

We had home advantage for the final that year and a massive chance to win our first title since 2000. Unfortunately Canterbury came to town and squeezed the life out of us. We sat in the sheds after a 7–6 defeat, wondering how we had come so far and failed at the final hurdle. The boys were letting the result sink in when I saw our manager, Dean O'Shaughnessy, wander over to coach Jamie Joseph. I couldn't hear the entire

We just got squeezed out in the 2008 Air New Zealand Cup final against Canterbury. Here, I'm about to soar above Colin Slade.

conversation, but I heard three things: 'Usual guys', 'Ross Filipo', and 'Cory Jane'.

A few minutes later, Jamie interrupted the commiserations to make an announcement. The All Blacks side was being officially announced the next day, but he had the list in front of him and wanted to officially congratulate the Lions boys who had made the team. He started by reading out the names of the current All Blacks — 'usual guys' — and then he announced Ross Filipo's name, which was greeted with massive cheers from the boys.

All the boys, that is, except me.

I had heard three things in Jamie's conversation with Dean. Now I had heard two of those three things again. Had I imagined hearing my name mentioned earlier? Was I dreaming this up? The next few seconds seemed to last a lifetime. The lads were still chahooing and carrying on for Rossco when Jamie Joseph read out one more name. 'Cory Jane.' Holy s—t! It was mine.

I had to be told that night that I had made the team because the following morning I would be meeting Graham Henry before the official announcement was made. There went the plans for a decent commiserations session with the boys. Instead it was back home to meet up with the family. Mum and Dad arrived, and Mum was in tears.

'Bloody hell, Mum,' I thought, 'it's not exactly something you should be crying about!' But it was a very emotional time for her.

I understood why when she sat down and told me a story. My poppa, her father, had passed away when I was 13, and though I didn't recall doing it, she said the last thing I did was leave a note in his casket. On that note was a simple message promising him that one day I was going to be an All Black. Following through on that promise obviously meant a lot to Mum.

Like all mums, mine holds on to everything. And she also blames everyone else. Dad refuses to go to games with her now because if I drop a ball, she'll blame the guy who passed it to me. If I miss a tackle, she'll blame someone else for not helping me. And this from a woman who tried to kill me on the postie bike.

I always have to remind her when I give her tickets to the games that all the other mums and dads will be sitting there, too, so she can't go slagging off their sons. She denies all knowledge of this of course, but it's the honest truth.

Mum is also a punisher when it comes to getting mementos for everyone. Mum will always be calling me to tell me that I have to get something signed, or get some kit for someone. I try to tell her that I'm too busy but she won't be dissuaded. 'You'll bloody do it,' she says. Needless to say, I just bloody do it.

While Mum was busy crying, Dad just wanted to sit down and have a beer. A handshake and a hug sufficed for the old boy.

It was a great night, for me and for the family, but the next day it would be down to business. I was nervous as hell going to bed that night, and I don't think I slept at all.

The next morning I found myself sitting next to the man who had picked me in the side.

Ted looked at me, and the first thing he said was, 'How did you sleep last night Cory?'

'Absolutely shocking,' I replied. 'I could barely sleep a wink, Ted.'

He paused for a moment, and then shot back, 'Sometimes sex helps.'

Too much info for Ted after the announcement of the All Blacks team at the end of 2008.

'Tried that,' I said, thinking I could speak freely.

He turned to me in disgust. 'Oh for God's sake, son, I don't want to hear about your bloody sex life.'

And that was my first conversation as an All Black. I knew immediately that I was going to love every second of it. With the pleasantries and pillow talk done, Ted simply told me that I had been picked for a reason and now it was up to me to go out there and do what I do. I couldn't wait to repay the faith. It's one thing to be picked as an All Black, it's another to get your first cap. That was now all I was focused on.

Ted isn't everyone's cup of tea, and he would be first to admit that, but I got on with him really well. I think after a career in education Ted knew enough about wayward schoolboys to understand what made them tick. He was for the most part accepting of the banter, but there were times when he had to bring out the verbal cane, and when he did you knew all about it.

I remember one session, a few years into my All Blacks career, vividly. We were setting up on defensive drills at Eden Park ahead of a Wallabies test. As a fullback I used to hate my wingers jamming in on defence, but when I was put on the wing I did exactly the same thing. I knew it was wrong, and of course the guys running the offence threw two passes and scored around my side of the field.

I was turning around to get back in position when from the other side of the field came the voice of Ted: 'Smithy, sort that bloody winger out.' Everyone in the team was staring at me. At the end of the training Smithy took me

'Smithy, sort that winger out!'

aside for a personal skills session, while the rest of the team watched the rookie learning some fundamentals.

On a tour to South Africa in 2009 we were practising kick-off receptions. The plan was the receiver would set a ruck and we would go from there. Tamati Ellison wasn't even looking when the first one was kicked to him and so he just put his hand up and called 'apologies' and everyone carried on. The next kick was aimed at me, but it went deep. Instinctively I trailed back, caught the ball, turned and kicked it into touch.

Ted spent the next five minutes breaking the record for the number of expletives used in a single training session. And all of them were aimed at me.

When the coach tells you to set a ruck, that's what you do! When they say there is nowhere to hide on a footy field, trust me, that's not just during a game. There's nowhere to hide at an All Blacks training session either. If there was, I'd probably still be hiding there.

Ted didn't mind bawling you out in front of everyone. That was just the way it was. I remember Willie Lose telling me a story about his time playing for Auckland. After a loss, Willie turned up to Eden Park training as always, said hello to Ted and got his gear on. Then he ran out onto the field, and warmed up with the team, as always. Then they were called into the huddle and split into forwards and backs. Willie, by this stage, had done a little bit of mental arithmetic and realised there was an extra forward at training. As the teams split into their groups, Ted yelled out in front of the entire team, 'Willie, what are you doing here? You're captaining the Bs. They're training at Avondale!'

After a quick discussion on the benefits of post-coital sleep with Ted, I was on the plane to Auckland to assemble with my first All Blacks side. It's weird packing for your first All Blacks tour because all you are told to bring is your belt, black shoes, underwear and toiletries. That's packing pretty light for a six-week tour of the UK!

I arrived in camp and was straight into one-on-one sessions with the coaches.

The one-on-ones are the most daunting meetings in all of rugby. The All Blacks coaches make a point every year of seeing you during the Super Rugby season, so you get hauled into a room and there's Steve Hansen and Ian Foster and Grant Fox, your trainers, the All Blacks trainers . . . they should change the name of the one-on-ones: they're more like eight-on-ones.

Most of the guys take their books in with them, but I can't do that. For starters, it's usually empty. Second, if I have a book in front of me I start doodling. I can't sit next to a window either, because I'll start looking out of it.

I can't tell you how often I have got halfway through a meeting and realised everyone's waiting for me to answer a question I never heard because I was watching some kid skateboard around the park.

I remember a couple of years ago I had come back from

a knee injury that had kept me out of the game for eight months. The only rugby I had had was a couple of ITM Cup matches followed by a couple of test appearances. Steve Hansen called me in for a catch-up — and when he calls you in for a catch-up, that's when you know you are going to be forced to play the word game.

The rules of the word game are simple. Shag, as he is known to all of us, is thinking of a word, and you have to figure out what it is. Synonyms don't count. You have to find the exact word he is thinking of otherwise you are going to be in there a long time.

Every coach has little tricks like this. The Crusaders boys often talk about Robbie Deans' habit of nodding while he talked. He kept nodding until you started nodding, too. Even if you didn't agree with a single thing

Robbie Deans . . . think before you nod.

he was saying, you'd find yourself nodding along. Richie McCaw says that more than once he had walked into the coach's office to take up an issue with Deansy, and walked out finding himself having nodded away for 20 minutes to the point where he had actually forgotten what it was he had come to talk about.

Yes, every coach has their own tricks, and Shag has the word game.

'CJ, you've been out a fair while son, so how are you feeling?' he asked me.

'I was a little gutted actually, Shag, I wanted to do a little better with my opportunities,' I told him.

'Yeah, but what *were* yuh, CJ?'

'I was disappointed, I was angry, I think I have let that anger get the better of me.'

'Yeah, but what *were* yuh, CJ?'

I must have talked for another 10 minutes, and after every attempt came the same response: 'Yeah, but what *were* yuh, CJ?'

There are only two ways the word game can finish. Either you hit the right word, or you ask Shag to tell you what it is. Finally, I was forced to give up.

'What do *you* think, Shag?' I finally said, knowing that my vocabulary had been maxed out.

'You were *frustrated*, CJ. You were *frustrated*.'

Well, I thought, if I wasn't before I certainly am now! There have been times when I've broken into a sweat during one of Shag's inquisitions. I've never enjoyed

'Yeah, but what *were* yuh, CJ?' Shag is the master of the word game.

getting up in front of other people to talk so when I find myself in the middle of a word game in front of others, I'm a wreck.

The one thing a one-on-one does teach you is this: it's okay not to know something. It takes you a while to figure this out as an All Black because the last thing you want to show is that you don't have an answer. The fact of the matter is there is something worse than not having an answer: being too afraid to ask a question.

With one-on-ones completed and the sweat on my forehead beginning to dry, it was off to my first All Blacks outfitting. Outfitting is the greatest thing ever for a kid from the Hutt. I walked into a giant hotel meeting room packed to the rafters with adidas kit. It was like a ticket to Santa's workshop.

Of course, I had no idea how it worked, so I stood for a while in the middle of the room and just stared at boxes of clothes and shoes.

At some point I walked over to a row of boxes filled with sunglasses and, again, I just stood there staring at them. Was I supposed to take a pair? What's the protocol?

I wasn't sure, but I bet it wasn't to stand as faux casually as I could looking the goodies up and down like a school kid in front of a lolly counter.

Finally the rep, sensing I was quite possibly the most uncomfortable man on the planet right then, offered some guidance. 'Pick some,' she said with a smile.

'Oh really, can we? Oh okay!' I said, pretending I had only just noticed that she was there. I grabbed a pair of new shades, and moved on to the next station, where I repeated the same awkward pantomime. I did this for half an hour at least, through the boots, and the shirts, and the shorts, and the shoes and the watches — by the end of it I understood why we packed light.

There is one last stop on your first outfitting circuit. This is when you get to try on for size the All Blacks jersey for the first time. I never thought the first place I would try on an All Blacks jersey would be in a meeting room at

FULFILLING A PROMISE

Ma'a leads the way at an All Blacks outfitting session.

the Heritage Hotel, but I tell you what, it felt good pulling it over my head.

I should say at this point that I had never been to an All Blacks test in my life. I had said as a child that the first All Blacks test I would go to would be the first one I played in. Now, here I was on the cusp of making that a reality, but I would have to wait at least another week. The first test of the tour was against the Wallabies in Hong Kong. Mils Muliaina was selected to play fullback and I wasn't named in the match day squad.

On the Thursday before the test, Ted came and sat down next to me in the team room. Mils' son Max was having some health problems and Mils had stayed in New Zealand to take care of his wee man. Ted stuck out his hand to shake mine, and simply said, 'Congratulations, you're on the bench for Saturday.' Then he got up and walked away.

I was still getting over the excitement of being handed a free watch and a pair of sunnies. Now I was going to be named in a test team.

In essence, when you get into the All Blacks camp for the first time, you realise you have been invited to join a very special club, and that leads to a lot of introspection. You are constantly questioning your value as a player and a person. 'Am I good enough to be here?' 'What do I have to do to make sure I am here for longer than one tour?' The All Blacks in one sense is a very comfortable place to be in terms of the support you get and the camaraderie of your

Relaxing with Snakey Smith after training in Hong Kong, 2008.

teammates, but you should never get too comfortable about your place in the mix.

That first week as an All Black was a strange experience for me. We had our own rooms in Hong Kong which is a rarity in the All Blacks, and in rugby in general, and it was certainly a novelty for me. Hong Kong was a new experience in so many ways. Even though I had been there once before with the sevens side, this was the first stop in my All Blacks career and it was quite overwhelming. I tried to keep calm by remembering what Ted had said: 'You were picked for a reason, go and do it.'

The Thursday night before my first test was a very lonely experience for me. I kept thinking of that strange axiom that says there's a difference between being picked in the All Blacks and playing for the All Blacks. I certainly felt that way in my heart, even though it was never spoken about.

Within the team your contribution is valued, regardless of whether you have played 80 tests or you are making your debut. Fostering a sense of contribution from everyone has been important in the team. It brings to life the words, 'You've been picked for a reason.' That would be a hollow statement if the culture was one of enforced silence for the rookies.

Receiving your test jersey is a great match day tradition. All Blacks manager Darren Shand had everyone's kit lined up in the team room and in I went to grab my socks, shorts and jersey from him. Once you have that test jersey it is your responsibility.

I have heard of guys leaving all sorts of things at the hotel on match day. Just look at Izzy Dagg: he keeps leaving his hair behind. But I have never heard of a single test player who has forgotten to pack his jersey.

I got so excited that I shook Shandy's hand and, being too impatient to wait for the lift, I ran up the stairs to my room. As soon as the door had clicked behind me, I had that full kit on and was standing in front of the mirror. Actually, that's not entirely true. I had taken a couple of minutes to do my hair first. You can't blame a man for wanting to look his best ahead of his proudest moment.

There was just one problem: my legs. I know I have mentioned them before but they really are abysmal. They're like two hairy twigs.

They stick out of the bottom of my shorts like a couple of straws that have been shoved up a set of nostrils. Brodie Retallick could floss his teeth with my legs. I even pulled the socks up to try to cover as much of them as possible.

After a couple of minutes . . . okay, after a good 20 minutes . . . oh, alright, after close to an hour of walking around my room posing in my test strip I just needed to shut down for a while. Having an attention deficit is not the greatest thing when you are as excited as I was about what was to come that night. I managed to doze a little before it was time to head downstairs, and onto the bus for my first test experience. It felt good thinking that this really would be my first test in every way. Having told myself as a child that the first All Blacks test I would go to would be the first one I played in suddenly didn't seem like the idle boasting of a cocky kid. It was now the truth.

5
TO TEST MATCH RUGBY & BEYOND

I WAS PRIMED for my first test match. All those years of trying to emulate my heroes on the practice field, all those smashed windows and cold mornings on the fields at Maoribank Park were now about to pay the ultimate dividend.

We arrived at the Hong Kong Stadium early, and I wasted no time getting out onto the paddock. Everyone has their own ritual when they arrive at a stadium. Some guys like to sit down and read the match programme, others like to get straight out onto the grass to get a sense of conditions and the surroundings. Andrew Hore and Jason Eaton liked to do a full lap of the ground before

CORY JANE — WINGING IT

Andrew Hore . . . the surname was always going to be a problem.

every match, although I always reckoned they were just planning where they were going to have their first beer that night.

It was amazing that both Jason and Andrew captained Taranaki. Wonderful, too, for stadium nicknames: when Jason was skipper, the boys knew Yarrow Stadium as 'the Pig Pen'. I don't think there's another stadium in the world that has been so well nicknamed after team captains: the Bull Ring, for Mark Allen, the Fish Bowl for Paul Tito. Unfortunately, given Andrew's surname, there was little choice: Yarrow became The Hore House.

I was so charged up for that game that my boots were on within a minute of arriving at the ground and I was straight into a warm-up. It was probably the greatest warm-up in test match history. I had been out on the field for an hour straight by the time the rest of the team came out. I don't think a bench player has ever worked up so much of a sweat before sitting on the pine for 75 minutes.

Every time the substitutes got up for a stretch during the match I had my jacket off and was ready to go.

I kept looking up at the coaching booth, believing somewhat naively that if I stared up there long enough, one of them might see me and put me on.

Soon after the break the first of the substitutions started rolling out. Every time Shandy came over I thought it was my chance to get out there. Fifty minutes passed, then 55. The final quarter arrived, then there were just 10 minutes left.

It was a strange sensation waiting for that first

opportunity. Keven Mealamu had been subbed in early when Andrew Hore had been injured, so there were only six of us left on the bench. Ma'a Nonu stripped in the forty-ninth minute, followed by Piri Weepu, then Greg Somerville and Anthony Boric. Adam Thomson went into the game with seven minutes to go. It suddenly dawned on me that I was the last one left. All I could think about was what it would be like in the sheds after the game knowing that I had come so close to a test debut, only to watch from the sideline.

With the clock ticking towards fulltime, Isaiah Toeava started cramping up. I'll admit it now, I almost started fist-pumping watching my own teammate on the ground as the medics tried to stretch him out. It sounds selfish

My final act of the Hong Kong test . . . a tackle on Wallabies winger Peter Hynes, which forced a turnover.

now, but I just wanted to get out there so badly. 'Ice' couldn't shake his cramp, and so the call finally came. I would have five minutes of the test.

Test match rugby is a collection of moments. The result of the match depends on how each of those moments is dealt with. My first touch in a test match was to catch a high ball. It was just a catch — a bread and butter play — but that first catch meant everything to me. Cory Jane 1, Test Rugby 0.

I was so glad I hadn't flubbed it that I turned to kick the ball back down field, and skied it off the side of my boot and straight into touch. Cory Jane 1, Test Rugby 1.

My final act of the game was to tackle winger Peter Hynes and force a turnover penalty. So, on balance, I figured I was ahead on the ledger. At fulltime we had won the game 19–14 and, with it, we had officially retained the Bledisloe Cup.

Those five minutes were so much better than the first time I had sex, and they seemed to last a bit longer, too. After the presentation the Bledisloe Cup was handed to me and Hosea Gear — who was also on debut — to walk it around the stadium. I don't know whether I was fatigued from my epic 90-minute warm-up, or drained by the adrenaline rush of taking the field in my first test, but that Cup was about the heaviest thing I have ever carried.

You can picture big, buff Hosea Gear on one side and me, the little runt of the pack, on the other. I don't know how many times I told him to stop so I could take a rest,

I'm smiling 'cos Hosea Gear is doing the heavy lifting after our 2008 Bledisloe Cup win in Hong Kong.

but each time he just told me to hurry up so we could get back to the sheds with the boys. I thought my arm was going to fall off by the time we got back to the tunnel.

It's a lovely touch to get the new boys to carry the Cup, and it's something that still happens to this day. I like to think that the idea is to make the new caps feel like part of the team, but I suspect all the veterans just know how much the thing weighs and they don't want to have to carry it themselves. As knackered as I was from the exertion of carrying rugby's biggest cup, I was buzzing when we got back inside.

After the game the handshakes all came with the same message: 'Welcome to the club.' That was in some ways more rewarding than hearing my name called out in the Wellington sheds, because from that day forward, no matter what happened, I had played a test for the All Blacks.

I had everyone sign my first test jersey. Some of them spelt my name wrong. I mean — really? The most cherished memento of my playing career has been signed to someone named 'Corey'. Mum's still furious about that.

Getting the congratulations from the likes of Dan and Richie was a great feeling, and then the new boys were presented with their first test tie. You get a new All Blacks formal tie on each tour, but you only ever get one 'first test' tie.

I was still pumped up as we boarded the bus that evening to head back to the hotel. On the way back,

Keven Mealamu and Rodney So'oialo called me down to the back seat. We had all grown up with stories about the pecking order on the team bus so I was fairly reluctant to heed the call, thinking that I was being put through some kind of rookie test.

I slowly made my way back, thinking at any moment something terrible would happen. By the time I got there I was as tense as a groom with second thoughts.

I looked at Kevvy and Rodney and, sure that I was about to take a pummelling, just came right out and said, 'Alright, what are you guys gonna do to me?'

Kevvy just looked at me like I was some kind of moron. 'What do you mean, CJ?' he asked.

'Well, I'm ready for yuh, just so you know,' I replied defiantly.

Kevvy and Rodney just looked at each other as if they had just heard the most stupid thing in their lives.

'No, CJ,' said Kevvy with a laugh. 'You've just played your first test so we wanted to welcome you!'

'Oh, okay then.' Jeez, I felt goofy.

It was a lovely moment for me, but the problem was I was left thinking Kevvy was nice all the time. It's true, Kevvy is one of the nicest men in the world, but every man has his limits, and trust me to find his.

In Hong Kong we each had our own rooms. In Scotland we would be sharing, and my first roomie was Kevvy. Emboldened by my experience on the bus I walked into my new digs. There was a double bed and a single bed and

Keven Mealamu . . . a gentle enforcer when it comes to team etiquette.

Kevvy's bags were on the double. This'll be good I thought to myself, and then I opened my big mouth.

'Heya, Kevvy,' I said to him as he turned from the window. 'Be a good man and just move that stuff for me there mate, ta.'

He looked me dead in the eye, like a Samoan Jack Palance. 'What did you say?' came his cold response.

I put my bags on the single bed and quickly left the room.

To be honest, though, he was a wonderful roommate and the best kind of guy to get to know on your first tour. There is no doubt he is the kaumatua of the team, and never was that more obvious than on the 2012 tour to South Africa.

There aren't many rules around what to wear and when to wear it in the All Blacks, but one thing that you do not do is wear a singlet to breakfast. It was the morning after the test match against the Springboks at Ellis Park and we had enjoyed a big win the night before. Izzy and I had seen Richie and Dan heading down to the hotel dining room in their singlets, so we just assumed this was a day in which the normal rules did not apply — an extended celebration of a good victory.

Once we saw the stars with their guns out, we just followed suit, and Izzy and I jumped in the lift in our singlets, all ready for a feed. As the doors opened on the ground floor, Kevvy was standing there.

'What you up to there, boys?' he asked, looking us up and down.

'Not much Kevvy, just heading to breakfast,' I replied.

He stood there for a moment, thinking about what to say.

'Okay, guys, do you think maybe you might want to go put a shirt on? Up to you, though. You guys decide if you think that's a good idea.'

There was no command, no overt instruction, but we both knew enough to read between the lines. Rules are rules and Kevvy, in his own calm way, was enforcing them — by putting the responsibility squarely on our (bare) shoulders.

We let the door close again and headed back to our rooms. A few minutes later, now properly attired, we both sat at breakfast thinking that there must be a different set of rules for the big boys in the team, seeing as we had earlier watched Dan and Richie walk down to breakfast in their singlets, while we were sent back to change.

How wrong we were.

We found out after our meal that Kevvy had been in the dining room when Dan and Richie arrived for breakfast and he had told them to go get their shirts on, because they wouldn't be eating until they did!

Richie is the skipper of the team and we all know that, but Kevvy's the man who sets the tone for the group. I don't think I've ever met anyone who is held in greater respect. He's the most humble guy, and he delivers the message in the most gentle way, but you know you'd better get that message loud and clear or you'll be facing some serious consequences. If Kevvy says you're not heading out after a test match, you're not heading out. If Kevvy says curfew is 2 am, you'd better be back in that hotel at 1.59.

Kevvy has a lot in common with Tana as a leader. If you do everything right, you'll never have a problem with them, and they'll never have a problem with you. Having endured a full Tana tirade early in my career, I don't ever want to be on the receiving end of one from Kevvy.

On tour, I often head to Kevvy's room. No, not for guidance counselling, but for the chance to beat him at *Madden*.

It'll come as no surprise to you that a lot of the boys are into their gaming on tour, and Keven Mealamu is no exception. Where he differs from the rest of us is that he is too damn humble. New Zealanders pilloried Australian cricketer Brad Haddin when he said, following the Cricket World Cup final, that the Black Caps were so nice it made him uncomfortable. But, anyone who has ever played *Madden* against Kevvy understands the sentiment.

Now, I can appreciate the reality of the graphics, the realistic simulation of NFL action and the outstanding user interface of the *Madden* franchise, but that's not why anyone challenges a teammate to a game.

The only good reason to challenge anyone to any kind of game is to give yourself the best opportunity to trash talk the hell out of them. And it is impossible to trash talk Keven Mealamu. Therein lies the problem.

The first thing to note here is that Kevvy won't let you into his room for a *Madden* session without your NFL jersey on, so it's one thing to remember to pack before you leave on tour. That's okay, a man has to have standards when it comes to dress codes (and we've already established that Kevvy has high standards). Once inside though, well, that's where the trouble starts. You see, Kevvy *knows* he's the best at *Madden*, and we all *kno*w he's the best at *Madden*, but even though he knows that we know that he knows, his humility is unbearable.

It happens all the time: he'll duly whip your ass and then . . . nothing. All he will do is politely thank you for the game, and when that happens your competitive subconscious starts to play tricks on you. You end up believing that what he is really saying is *you are terrible, now get out and don't come back until you've got some game*. All you can do after that is skulk off to your room.

And it's even worse on those rare occasions when you win. Again, all he will do is politely thank you for the game, and he does it in such a humble and genuine way that you are effectively prevented from celebrating the victory by the traditional method which, of course, is to rub it in mercilessly until your opponent is forced to walk away.

If I beat anyone at anything, I'm going to let them know about it, for at least a couple of days, but Kevvy, through his insufferable graciousness, never gives anyone that chance.

You can see the problem here. When a guy reacts that way to defeat, you immediately realise that you would have reacted in the complete opposite fashion, which in turn means you ultimately know he's a better person than you. In your moment of triumph, he's managed to make you feel terrible, which is just not right.

On tour, Kevvy is Mr Gadget. He's a one-man entertainment system — PlayStation, projector, you name it, Kevvy will have it. For that reason alone, his room is always a good place to chill out. But only if you can drag a couple of other boys in there to trash talk at the same time.

6
ON WITH THE JOB

YOU ALWAYS HAVE TO re-evaluate your goals, both in life and sport. For me, that re-evaluation came almost immediately after I had left the stadium in Hong Kong. I had achieved a lifelong dream and played in a test for the All Blacks, but now I had to make a decision: did I want to be a one-test All Black or a 50-test All Black? You have to recognise that certain talents and abilities get you so far and the things that will get you further are hard work and increased dedication. Once you are welcomed into that club, you never want to leave. At least, that's how I felt. That's how I still feel.

I was on the bench the following week against Scotland and again Isaiah Toeava's misfortune was an opportunity for me to get game time. Ice had taken a stinger just before halftime and wasn't able to get back into the game.

Showing off my soccer skills at training in Edinburgh a couple of days out from the test against Scotland in 2008.

I thought straight away about Hong Kong: if that's what five minutes feels like, imagine how much fun I could have with a whole half!

Playing at Murrayfield is a fantastic experience. Edinburgh is a great city to visit, and the stadium experience is epic in scale. It's surreal when they turn the lights out and the lone piper appears on the roof. I had to ask Joe Rokocoko to smile so I could see what I was doing. Listening to the anthem and hearing the singing — it's one of the iconic test match experiences, and that first taste of it is a memory I'll cherish forever.

I remember that game well because Stephen 'Beaver' Donald and I completely bombed a try with the line beckoning and no one in front of us. Liam Messam had made a bust and I had called on the outside for the pass.

Beaver hadn't heard me call and he came rushing up like a gangly Clydesdale, reaching for a pass which proved just too tough for him to catch, but which would have been just perfect for me.

We both looked at each other after the knock-on, and it was all we could do not to laugh.

The result in Edinburgh was never in doubt so, in the greater scheme of things, it didn't really matter. But, it's these little moments that count when your personal contribution is being analysed by the coaches. That was certainly a moment we both would have loved to have taken back. And there was another, two years later, as well . . .

Reviews are terrifying at the best of times, but there

are days when you wish you had worn your bulletproof vest. When the guns start going off you just hope it's not you in the firing line. Unfortunately there is nowhere to hide, as Beaver and I found out after the 2010 test loss against Australia in Hong Kong.

After our long trip to England following the Hong Kong test, the coaches were in no mood to go easy on us. Hong Kong was a loss that hurt because it shouldn't have happened. To lose like that, in the final minute of the game, wasn't just a defeat, it was an attack on our ability to finish a job — something we pride ourselves on in the All Blacks.

It was also the worst kind of way to start a tough tour. There wasn't a lot of talk as we all gathered and waited for the onslaught to begin. And, boy, did it begin.

Soon enough it was my turn to be singled out. At one stage in the game we had taken a 22-metre drop-out. It was Reado's job to catch it . . . my job to catch it if he couldn't. Sure enough, he missed it and I caught it but then, sensing I was about to be tackled into touch, I had kicked it as hard as I could downfield. Australia brought it out of their backfield and set up phase play in our half, and even though it didn't lead to a scoring play, the coaches had already loaded up.

'What were you doing here, CJ?' Ted barked at me. All the eyes in the room were now fixed on yours truly. Again I could feel those telltale beads of sweat beginning to form and swell on my forehead. I fumbled for a response.

Ted offers me some practical advice on when to kick and when to kick! I got a hell of a spray after my effort in Hong Kong.

'Well, I was about to go into touch, so I thought it would be better to give us a chance upfield than play a defensive lineout 30 metres from our own line,' I replied.

'Did you now, CJ?' Ted responded in a voice that would wither a plastic pot plant.

'Well, that would have been a good idea, IF THAT WAS THE F--KING PLAN!'

I just wanted the floor to open up and swallow me, but there was another barrage coming, and this time for another mistake from a kick-off. Ted and the other coaches didn't miss with that shot, either. And I just had to sit there in a cold and clammy sweat, taking the bullets. The only positive thing about the experience was that Beaver got it even worse, but we both walked out of that room at the end of the meeting wondering what had just hit us.

We've all had moments like that in reviews and one thing I will say is this: there's no pecking order in a review session. It doesn't matter if you're a 100-test veteran, a one-test rookie, or the captain of the side; if you are not taking care of the details on Saturday you'll be in the line of fire on Monday. A metre off your run line? Bang! Slow to get back on defence? Crack! Kicking the ball downfield when you were supposed to run it? Boom!

I don't mind being told when I have had a bad game, and you learn very quickly that only by taking care of the smallest details can you expect to win test matches. When you are sitting in that room getting filleted like a gurnard, you become very aware of the faces of the guys around you — and on all of those faces is the same look. No, it's not sympathy, it's 'Thank f--k it's him and not me.'

I say there is nowhere to hide in the review, but that hasn't stopped blokes in the past.

Izzy Dagg would always try to hide down the back, but he was easy to spot because the light would be bouncing off his bald spot.

The best thing to do is to find a spot directly behind someone like Brodie Retallick, hoping that you'll be shielded by the enormous bulk and rendered completely invisible to the coaches in the front.

Over the last few years the policy has changed so that the starting team fills the front row, which is good for the rest of the squad because they can enjoy the carnage from a safe distance. It's pretty much the only good thing about not starting a test.

That said, even if I wasn't starting a test it would be just like the coaches to go back to Thursday and blame me for something I did during a defensive drill at training.

There's often a strange reverse proportionality during review sessions, too. If the game has been close, you know the heavy artillery is coming out but, oddly, if the boys have played really badly and the game has been a shambles, it is almost as if the mercy rule is invoked: the coaches know that we are all aware of the fact we have failed — individually and collectively — to get the job done, and realise that they probably don't have to finish us off with a couple to the head. Interestingly those are probably the sessions that hurt the most, because that's when you know the coaching staff are really pissed off at you.

Of course, you do have a chance to fire back if you think you have enough ammo, but you had better make sure you're on target, especially with Shag. It may be a genetic thing, I'm not sure, but Shag is never wrong. He is the wise tortoise of the All Blacks. For this reason, it's rare that one of the boys will get one over him. However, Jamie 'Whoppa' Mackintosh did a pretty good job of it on the 2008 tour. It was a very funny joke, but sadly not one I can share in a family friendly publication.

Shag the wise tortoise.

Whoppa had been appointed to the music committee, which was a brave decision from the leadership group given that he's from Invercargill. Invercargill's the only town in New Zealand where Suzanne Prentice could run for mayor tomorrow on the strength of the fact her songs are still on high rotate on the local radio station. I'm not saying Invercargill is backward, but this is the kind of town where people rewind their CDs.

The rules of the music committee are fairly simple: if you're on the bus and the music is not playing, you have to fill in the silence by singing, or by telling a joke.

Whoppa went for the joke, and made Shag the butt of it. It was great to see Whoppa get a rare victory over Shag. None of us have ever been able to figure out why it is Whoppa only got one test cap.

I knew the Scotland test in 2008 would be my last of the season. Mils Muliaina had rejoined the squad and I knew I hadn't done enough to take either his or Isaiah Toeava's place in the test team. My next focus would have to be the match against Munster, and I don't think we quite knew what we were getting ourselves in for.

For starters, when someone tells you the place you're heading for is called 'Stab City' you start to wonder whether the adventure was a good idea in the first place. Maybe that's unfair to Limerick but, still, you don't get a reputation like that unless there's a little bit of smoke with the fire. I should have known better than to buy into that sort of hype.

After all, everyone thinks Upper Hutt is full of bogans but, as any Upper Hutt native knows, you won't find a more civilised and urbane population anywhere in New Zealand. You shouldn't judge a book by its cover, I always say. And you can't in Upper Hutt anyway, because no one reads them.

The 2008 Munster game loomed large on the tour because of the novelty factor. We were all aware that this would be the first midweek fixture the All Blacks had played for a long time. In fact, it had been seven years since the side had played one, and 11 years since a match against a famous provincial or regional side. It was also the thirtieth anniversary of the famous 1978 Munster victory over the All Blacks, a victory that put a slight dampener on that side's historic first-ever grand slam

The Kiwi boys in the Munster side set the tone for the home team back in '08 with this haka. In shot are, from left, Rua Tipoki, Doug Howlett and Lifeimi Mafi.

win. We were on a grand slam quest of our own, and we were in no mood for a repeat of the wrong kind of history.

We may have been in 'Stab City' but it was us who had brought a knife to this particular gunfight. One thing about playing for the All Blacks is that you come to expect opposition teams will invariably grow an extra arm, and maybe a couple of legs as well. That's the way it was that night against Munster.

Right from the beginning we knew we were going to be in for a torrid evening at Thomond Park. To be on the receiving end of a haka, when Doug Howlett, Rua Tipoki, Lifeimi Mafi and Jeremy Manning laid down the challenge on Munster's behalf, was something none of us had ever experienced. It set the tone for the match, but perhaps more for the home side than for us.

It is an unsettling thing to be in the middle of a stadium filled to capacity and to feel it go silent, as Irish crowds do when kickers are taking shots. I can't even get four kids to keep quiet for longer than five seconds; how the Irish manage this is beyond me, but I want to know the secret.

It was the first time I had stood in the middle of a deathly quiet stadium, and I was glad it was Beaver taking the kicks and not me.

We only just scraped through that match — how, I don't know — but we were hugely relieved. In hindsight, we took them lightly. We tried to compare the match with the All Blacks playing a club team from back in New Zealand, but what we hadn't counted on was the fervour and the passion of the home support. That match made me fall in love with the spirit of the northern hemisphere supporters, and it is something I will never forget. Doug Howlett gave me his jersey at the end of the match. I treasure that jersey.

We were lucky, and we knew it, but very little was said in the sheds after that match. Nothing needed to be said. Games like that, against Munster, or Italy and the Barbarians the following year, teach the rookies about what it takes to stay calm, and to stay on plan. When you are new to the environment you just want to play, so when you get the chance you can't help but show a little too much exuberance, a little too much enthusiasm.

When you get over-hyped you forget to do your job

Happy and relieved in the dressing room after the Munster match. I'm flanked by Hika Elliot and Munster Kiwi Jeremy Manning.

and, in the All Blacks, that's what you have to do: your job. You have to trust the other boys to do theirs.

That trust in each other's abilities is one of the key reasons the All Blacks are so successful and, conversely, when you have a match like we did against Munster, and get a win by the skin of your teeth, you learn very quickly that when that trust goes, things go south at a rapid rate.

As All Blacks, we are under scrutiny at Super Rugby level, and when form drops off, or is perceived to have dropped off, you can almost always trace it back to the fact that you are trying too hard. You end up like Bryan Adams' band back in 1969. If you asked any Super Rugby champion what the key to victory was, they would tell you it was trust in each other's ability, and everyone in the team sticking to their roles. Trust is the hardest thing to develop in a side, which is why the All Blacks treasure it.

Despite the fact we only just scraped through against Munster, that game will always stay with me for the valuable lesson it provided us all.

The summer of 2009 was a great time to reflect. But it was also a time for me to get better. It was nice to think I had played in two test matches and the Munster game. Still, I wasn't satisfied with a spot on the bench. Don't get me wrong; making the match day squad was, and still is, a great privilege, but every All Black wants to be starting the party, not rolling in halfway through. In some ways, a test match is like a concert in reverse: the headline act is on stage at the beginning, and the support acts close the night. I wanted to feel what it was like to be the headline act.

In June 2009, I would get my chance. And it would change my career forever.

7

WINGING IT & THE RISE OF THE BOMB SQUAD

I WAS SELECTED for the All Blacks again for the June series against the French in 2009. Rudi Wulf and Joe Rokocoko had been listed on the wings, and Mils Muliaina had been chosen to captain the side for the first test at Carisbrook. I was once again named on the bench, until Rudi damaged his shoulder in training after landing awkwardly while catching a high ball. It seems high balls would go on to define our All Blacks careers, but for very different reasons. As it was, once again, a teammate's misfortune was my opportunity.

Sure enough, Rudi's injury meant I was elevated to start, and I would be playing on the left wing. Now I don't

High hopes as I run out onto Carisbrook for my first starting match for the All Blacks, against the French in 2009.

know whether I was naive, cheeky or just a bit simple, but I figured I would prefer the right wing, so I asked Joe Rokocoko to swap with me. I'm not entirely sure that is standard operating procedure in the All Blacks, but it was fine in the Rimutaka under 6s, so I just did it. Joe certainly didn't mind — he was a natural left wing anyway and had only swapped to the right because Rudi was an out-and-out leftie.

Whether it was the done thing or not, it was a done deal. I would start my first test in the unfamiliar role of right wing, even though I still played in the number 11 jersey. I must have gone alright, too, even though we lost that game.

The Carisbrook sheds were a depressing enough place to be anyway — imagine a Second World War air raid shelter crossed with a milking shed — but on that night I finally understood the enormity of the responsibility of playing for your country. A whole country is an awful lot of people to let down.

After a win the shed is a great place to be. The boys are full of chat and are having a good time. When you lose, it's sombre. No one wants to look another person in the eye. The only place with less eye contact than a losing All Blacks side's shed is a hall hosting a Year 8 social.

I had lost plenty of games before, but none of this magnitude. I sat in the sheds and thought about the fact the whole country was gutted about our performance that night. I may have let down my parents, and my school teachers, and a few other people in life, but letting down a nation? That's something you should leave to politicians.

We know what kind of level we can play at as All Blacks, and we put a lot of pressure on ourselves to reach that level each and every time we play a match. We know, too, that our fans expect us to perform under that pressure so, when we don't, we know they'll be gunning for us. In some ways you have to experience a loss to understand just how much it hurts.

In saying that, I didn't want to experience that feeling again, and neither did anyone else in the side. And so, as Shag once so eloquently put it, we flushed the dunny and moved on. Thank goodness I wasn't flushed with it.

Truth is, a part of me *was* flushed that day — the part that aspired to be an All Blacks fullback. The die was cast, my fate was sealed; if I was going to make a name for myself as a test player, it was going to be on the wing.

If the sheds are awkward after a loss, the following week is just as bad. The coaches redouble their efforts around analysis and tactics, and as a result the talk is kept to a minimum. The one bonus of this is that Shag doesn't bother playing the word game; he just tells you what the word is and tells you to get on with the job.

That job involved getting to Wellington and winning a test match. It would be a special moment for me as it was my first chance to play on my home ground in front of my family and friends. And for the week leading up to the game I was put in a room with Brad Thorn.

Brad Thorn always sat at the back of the bus and was the team music sheriff. You can imagine in a team like the All Blacks there are some fairly diverse musical tastes. Needless to say there are plenty of hip-hop aficionados, there's the Crusaders' country and western club, and Richard Kahui, the human jukebox, who knows the words to every song ever written. Ted was also a big music fan, though none of us ever knew what he listened to because he never let us borrow his discman. And then there was Brad Thorn, for whom only rock would do.

It didn't matter what song went on, or who was running the music committee; if it wasn't a rock anthem on the playlist you could be guaranteed to hear the same gravelly line from the back seat: 'Turn that shit off!'

Thorny always called me Little Cobra on account of my appalling attempts to flare up in the gym. The big man

The Little Cobra tracks Big Brad at All Blacks training.

would just start laughing. 'Hahaha! Little Cobra! You're just a very little man, CJ.' Then he would deadlift a fridge and walk off with his pectorals bouncing up and down like pistons.

He was the guy who had played forever — and looked like it. I always thought he was in his mid-fifties when we were in the All Blacks together. And he was never shy of ripping you to shreds. Thorny may have been a Christian, but he didn't worship at the altar; he worshipped at the squat machine and the bench. He loved chucking tin and couldn't understand how anyone else wouldn't.

On more than one occasion, my best effort was greeted with the immortal line, 'CJ! If you are not going to lift proper tin, just get out of the gym!'

I would be straining on a bench press and he'd be spotting me with his index finger, laughing, and asking me when I would be finished my warm-up.

If he wasn't lifting he would be stretching, and you always — always — had to wait for him after training until he had finished his stretching session. We'd all be on the bus and the old fella would be in some strange yoga pose on the grass. Not that anyone felt like telling him to hurry up. And, besides, whatever he did it obviously worked considering he retired well into his sixties.

Thorny was the consummate trainer, and he knew all the tricks. At team lunches he would always order a fizzy drink, knowing full well that no nutritionist was going to tell him he couldn't. Ever since I first saw that, I have

The tin men. Above, me on my 'warm-up' and, below, Big Brad on his 200th rep!

ordered a fizzy at every team lunch as well. If it was good enough for Brad Thorn, it was good enough for the Little Cobra.

He was a hard man, too, and he never backed down. There were plenty of times when the coaches would tell him to work on something and he would look them in the eye and say, 'It's rugby, all I have to do is smash people.'

He never got too caught up in the finer details, and the coaches never really felt the need to overcomplicate things for him. I can just imagine how well it would go down if I took the Thorn approach to being told to work on something. Put it this way, I wouldn't be playing in the next test.

Despite being the new kid on the block, I immediately fell in love with taking the piss out of the lads. I was, and still am, an equal opportunities piss-taker. I don't play favourites, which means I am loathed equally by everyone in the team. Actually, that's not entirely true; I don't have a crack at the captain. But he hates me as well.

Apart from the fact he would probably make sure I never played again, there is a serious reason not to give the Skip shit: he's got enough going on. I mean, look at that hairstyle.

After a second test win over France in Wellington, and a scrappy victory against Italy in Christchurch, the 2009 season moved on to Eden Park. This is where I had my first, and last (I think) awkward moment with the skipper.

Things were a little slow on the Wednesday of the test

Richie's the skipper. If *he* points, *I* point.

build-up so I thought I would head to the hotel restaurant for team lunch. As I walked in I saw that there was only one other guy at the table, the skipper, Richie McCaw. Let me just explain something here: I'm never afraid of a chat, but when your All Blacks career is all of six months' old, having to spend lunch engaged in a one-on-one with the great man is a daunting prospect. I was just about to make a bolt for the door, but it was too late, McCaw had spotted me with the eye in the back of his head.

There was nothing for it. I had to go and sit down with him and have a chat. But what was I going to go and talk to him about? Don't get me wrong, I can hold my own conversationally, as long as that conversation involves immature put-downs and banal topics to debate. I sensed this was not going to be one of *those* conversations. I grabbed a breath mint off the counter (just in case he wanted a kiss) and made my way to the table.

'How are you going there, Skip?' I said, trying to sound confident.

'Good Cory. You?'

'Nah. Good.'

Awkward pause.

'So how's things?'

'All good, CJ, just the usual week mate.'

Awkward pause.

'So, are you still doing your gliding, then Skip?'

'Yep, I like to fly mate.'

I had no idea what to say next. I had probably had four small spoonfuls of whatever was on my plate, and I just had to tell the skip I wasn't hungry any more, got up, and left as fast as I could. All I could think on the way back to the elevator was, I'll never play for the All Blacks again.

At least Richie didn't take offence. He probably walked back to the elevator wondering who the complete simpleton was who had sat down next to him at lunch.

Fortunately, whatever he thought he kept to himself because I kept getting picked in the All Blacks. And, of course, our conversations are a bit easier these days.

We got the win over the Wallabies at Eden Park, and headed to South Africa for two tests in Bloemfontein and Durban. We were handed a lesson in both test matches. The Springboks peppered us with high balls, and we had

Smithy and Mick 'The Kick' Byrne formulating plans for the bomb squad.

no real strategy for getting ourselves out of the backfield.

Catching the kick is one thing, and I guess I made a name for myself as someone who could gobble up the high balls. But catching them is often the easy part; as we soon began to realise, it's what you do after the catch that counts.

The two tests in South Africa got Wayne Smith and skills coach Mick 'The Kick' Byrne thinking. They realised that if we wanted to make the most of the possession from kicks, we needed to focus attention on how the back three operated as a trio under bomb pressure. It was something that none of us as players had really thought about, but we began to make it a major focus at training. Smithy, as he likes to do, discovered a new toy, and imported a giant 'turtle' shield that he would put on his back for us to jump up and leverage our height from. Mick, who had made a name for himself as an AFL player, was the master of the detail.

If we wanted to have a good structure around the high ball, the guys closest to the receiver had to know what to do in terms of getting around the ball carrier and ensuring possession was retained. Once that was done, we had the ability to turn a defensive play into a phase from which to launch an all-out assault.

When you are lining up a catch under chase pressure, every microsecond counts and nowadays every team has a strategy in place.

The alignment of players upfield from the kick receiver can be the difference between successfully gaining possession or being annihilated by a tackle.

It was a masterclass in coaching. Truth is, you can coach all the skills you like, but each of those skills requires the combination, before and after, of another set of skills. You can break things down to real detail, but the best coaches offer that detail with context. There is no point, for instance, being the best catcher in the game if your teammates don't get their alignment right, and your support crew doesn't know how to clean a ruck. That's what we practised more than anything — the before and after were as important as the now.

With a new focus on the kick receipt as a strategic attacking weapon, as opposed to a standard defensive play, all wingers suddenly had to be good exponents of the high ball catch. And that's where the interchangeability of

WINGING IT & THE RISE OF THE BOMB SQUAD

Catch 22, or 33, or 44, or however many it took to make us good exponents of the high ball catch.

My first try for the All Blacks, against Australia in Wellington, 19 September 2009.

the All Blacks back three really began. Suddenly it made sense to have players who were comfortable as both wings and fullbacks. The line between the positions was blurred by the need to operate under the high ball.

The South Africans had done their best to expose the All Blacks wingers under the high ball in that 2009 series. Sitiveni Sivivatu and Joe Rokocoko were our starting wingers and the Springboks were relentless in their targeting of them. I think, more than anything, having the ability to catch high balls was my greatest weapon, and it was a weapon that was required at precisely that time in the continual evolution of the game. As they say, right time, right place.

By the time we hit the end of year tour in 2009, everyone in the back three was clear on what needed to be done, and we

Imploring Zac Guildford to keep his clothes on at training.

would get plenty of opportunity to implement the strategy in the test against Wales at Millennium Stadium. We knew the Welsh would make it rain high balls, and we were confident we could make the tactic work to our advantage.

I was selected to play on the right wing, and Zac Guildford was picked to make his debut on the left. Zac would make any troublesome XV named in the world.

He loved being nude, so when you roomed with him you just had to get used to hanging out, talking to a naked dude. It's not as easy as you think to be discussing plays and tactics with a guy who's just lounging around the room in the buff. I don't know why he's so averse to wearing clothes but, hey, good for him.

The only other man I know who has his clothes off as much as Zac is the lesser known of the two Hurricanes legal experts, Victor Vito. He would be the hardest man in the world to drag away from the mirror. Not since Willie Lose has a Polynesian player had such a love affair with his own reflection. You can tell if it's been raining because Vic walks with his head down to catch a look at himself in the puddles. For all his smarts, Vic still has never seen what's on the other side of a window.

Vic loves taking his top off. And he does it everywhere — at trainings, in meetings, during lunch. If he could play the game shirtless, he would.

He's even considered getting his number tattooed on his back just in case one day he'll be allowed to take the field half nude. Only problem with that is his back's not quite big enough for the number '20'.

Vic is a man who has such big raps on himself, we have to give him plastic cutlery because if you gave him a normal spoon he would never get past the soup course. He'd spend the whole time wondering why his face was all out of proportion. Vic is hard to wind up, because he thinks he's smarter than the rest of us, but if you ever want to see him arc up, just call him fat. He won't talk to you for days.

Vic has one other major issue: he talks like a white guy. Every once in a while it would be good to hear him call us 'bro', but he never will. The only thing Vic takes more seriously than how he looks is how he sounds.

Vic Vito was never going to turn down the chance to model for Jockey.

Back in Wales, Zac and I talked about the high ball plays all week (his balls were out anyway so it made sense) and we made a pact to catch every single kick that came our way. We decided that, if we were going to set ourselves a mission, we definitely needed a name. That week, we became the Bomb Squad.

I still pride myself on catching high balls. I get more frustrated if I drop a high ball than I do making any other error in the game. Luckily I haven't dropped one for 32 years, but if I did . . .

8
FASHION & TANS

LET US CONSIDER the notion of rugby IQ. Okay, I know I'm not the best person to talk about IQ of any sort, but the simple truth is a lot of players aren't blessed with rugby brains. I may have spent my school days staring into space and pretending to be someone else to sneak into PE class, but on a rugby field I like to think I am fully engaged with what is going on. Some players, on the other hand, are rugby savants, and I admire them all. Usually they go on to be great coaches, too. I can think of guys like Tana Umaga, Aaron Mauger and Daryl Gibson to name just a few.

It's all about scanning for opportunities — defensively and offensively. If a team has a lineout throw, I am watching the first-five for cues about where the attack is coming from. Who is he talking to? Where is he standing? Where is the fullback, the wing, the midfielders? Where are they looking?

Since moving to the wing I have always prided myself on communicating with my fullback — whether that is

Izzy Dagg or Bender Smith in the All Blacks, or guys like Andre Taylor and Nehe Milner-Skudder at the Hurricanes. It is my job to cover the right. It is their job to be ready for what's coming their way. Ahead of us, it is the job of forwards to put pressure on the lineout, then to put pressure on the kick. My job is to catch the ball, and then my back three partners are ready to attack from the next breakdown.

The All Blacks are a big kicking team, but we try to only kick for wins. Simply put, if you kick the ball and the opposition catch it, you have failed. If you kick and they drop it, that's a win. If you kick and you turn them over, that's a win. If you kick and find space, that's a win. If you kick and catch on a chase, that's a *big* win. It's all about doing your job, and having your team do their jobs at the same time.

If I could have seen schoolwork like I see a rugby field there is no doubt I'd have a whole lot of letters after my name right now.

I don't mean that as a statement of arrogance, but I am always amazed at how I can see the patterns and plays, how I can think three moves ahead, and how I can anticipate the action on a rugby field. I can do all that, but I can't find 'hippopotamus' in the dictionary.

Hurricanes coach Chris Boyd has said more than once that he can't believe how well I can read a game of footy when I can't even read the team noticeboard.

When I am out on the field, and not getting any ball, I am visualising what I will do when I do get the ball, so

FASHION & TANS

Chris Boyd . . . recognises talent when he sees it.

that when it happens I have already worked out a plan of attack. That's the best way to be because if you have to start thinking when you have the ball, you are going to be cluttered.

You have to back your skills, and for me that is getting my footwork in place and getting myself into a position to fend. I'm not the kind of guy who is going to bump people off. I wish I was but I'll leave that to the likes of Julian Savea. If he's 'The Bus' then I'm the 'Smart Car'. For me, it is about creating the mismatch through deception, by making a defender take a step in the wrong direction or back off you just a little bit too far.

People ask me how I learned to fend, or how I learned to step, but the answer is not complicated: it's the way I have always played the game, because it plays to my strength. Even back on the field at Maoribank Park with the Rimutaka under-6s I learnt the best thing I could do was to run away from people, not run into them.

Rugby teams require great game managers in key positions, and in the most key position of all there is probably none more effective than Dan Carter.

Dan is the only Crusader I know who gives a damn about fashion, but he's gone so far the other way that we're all a little worried about him. I learnt the hard way in 2010 that you need to have three beds when you room with him: one for him, one for you, and one for his toiletries bag.

The first time I ever roomed with him I had to step around his toiletry bag to get to the shower. I don't know how he gets it on the plane without paying excess baggage fees.

In fact, knowing him, he's probably got those fees written into his contract.

Don't get me wrong: Dezzy is a good-looking man who obviously cares about taking care of his appearance, but it's a fine line between having a beauty regime and running what amounts to a portable commercial cosmetics warehouse. He has to take his toothbrush and comb out as soon as he arrives at a new hotel otherwise he would have to spend most of the week searching for it amongst his collection of wrinkle creams, cooling gels, body lotions, lip balms, essential oils, exfoliating scrubs and moisturisers.

The last time I had seen an All Black applying anything

FASHION & TANS

Dezzy Carter . . . fashion icon and cosmetics for all occasions.

other than soap and water to his face was the first time I saw Ma'a Nonu putting on eyeliner. I didn't know what to think. I had been heading to my room after being strapped for a match, and I walked past his open door right at application time.

There is a certain level of comfort a man must have to leave his door wide open while he is doing his lashes. I must admit, I was a little taken aback. I didn't want to say anything — you should never interrupt a man while he's applying make-up — and, to be quite honest, the more I looked the more I thought it did go rather well with the blond tips on his dreads.

Ma'a must be the most misunderstood man in the professional era of New Zealand rugby. He is an exceptionally funny man, or at least he thinks he's funny.

This is helped by the fact he always travels with a Polynesian posse, and he has taught them to laugh at everything he says. Once you're surrounded by the laughing Samoans there is no comeback; you just have to go find a white guy to pick on to make you feel better. Preferably a Crusader. Better still, Wyatt Crockett.

That first time I roomed with Dezzy, I couldn't help but mention the impressive size of his . . . toiletries collection. He turned to me with a smile and asked if I would like to have a go after him.

'Aw, nah, it's alright Dan, I'm not much into moisturising,' I told him.

'No, CJ, do you want to have a go on this after me?'

FASHION & TANS

Julz thinks it's funny, but Ma'a only laughs when *he's* telling the joke.

He was pointing at a box that had just arrived in the room. And blow me down if it wasn't his own portable sun bed.

I had always wondered — as you probably have, too — how Dezzy managed to keep that year-round glow. I mean, I'm top drawer in the summer — a nice, healthy tan, a spring in my step — but in winter, well, I'm about as pasty as an albino narwhal. I could never figure out how Dezzy managed to always look like he'd just stepped off some beach scene in *Home and Away*. Now, I knew.

'So, you want a go after me, CJ?' he asked again.

I looked at the machine and back at him. 'Jeez, Dan,' I ventured. 'I'd probably burn up, wouldn't I?

'We'll just give you a few minutes mate, and see how you go.'

It was a nice offer but unfortunately once bitten twice

shy. I had already had one sunbed experience and that was one too many.

It was the boy's day off ahead of the 2009 England test at Twickenham and Tamati Ellison, my old Mana College nemesis, wandered into the team room. He took one look at me, hollered me over and simply said, 'CJ, we need to go get us some.'

I was wondering what the hell he was talking about. Things got more bizarre when he put his hands up to his eyes to make the international sign for goggles. I was trying to figure out what sort of place he wanted to take me to: an underwater strip club, perhaps? Noticing the blank look on my face, he gave up the charade and said, rather matter-of-factly, 'We need to go and get a sunbed.'

Two things here: one, Tamati is Maori. I thought their tans were kind of permanent. Two, one sunbed was not going to do much for me.

Never one to take no for an answer, Tamati could not be dissuaded from the mission. Off we went through the streets of Kensington, looking for a tanning salon. Sure enough — and why was I not surprised — we soon found one.

'So, do you use sunbeds often,' the receptionist asked me as we waited. I was wearing jeans and a hoodie at the time. Had I not been, that question would have been rendered redundant, and she probably would have recommended I avoid treatment altogether. As it was, not wanting to look silly, I told her I did, and she locked me in for the full 12 minutes.

I don't want to judge people who use sunbeds, but all I will say is this: if you ever want to know what a chicken would feel like if you rotisseried it live, then go and lie in a sun bed for 12 minutes. If Wyatt Crockett did that he would walk out covered in crackling.

That night I had a full body massage booked. I stripped off to get onto the table and Tamati started pissing himself laughing. I was the kind of red that would make a tomato blush. And I was red ALL OVER. I got on the table and I could tell the masseuse was wondering what the hell was going on.

'You are very red, Cory,' she said. I didn't know what to say. Tamati was giggling like a schoolgirl on the bed next to me.

All I could think of was that it was a lie that got me into this mess. I didn't want to make that mistake again.

And then I did.

'Yeah, I ate some peanuts earlier and I think it might be a reaction to those,' I told her.

It was the most painful massage of my life. It wasn't a rub down, it was a belt sanding. I was in agony. The massage lasted all of five minutes, before I had to pull the pin. Somewhere in the UK, there's still a massage therapist telling people about the time she worked on an All Black with a painful peanut allergy.

Next time, I promised I would just do what the Welsh do, and get painted orange.

Tanning is one thing, tattooing is another altogether, and there are plenty of tough stickers in the All Blacks side. Izzy even got his surname tattooed across his back, just in case he ever forgot who he was. Only problem is, now every time he looks in a mirror he thinks his name is Israel Ggad.

Unfortunately, Hikawera Elliot decided to become the team's impromptu tattooist on a flight to Hong Kong at the end of the 2010 northern tour. Now Hika — aka Sickawera or the Hikapotamus, is probably the one man who can piss people off faster than I can, and he is always up for a bit of stirring.

Hika thought it would be a good idea to give a few of the boys marker pen mokos after they fell asleep. He picked out two targets: Isaiah Toeava and Jerome Kaino.

Now, I owed Isaiah already. Without him cramping up and breaking down in 2008 I may never have got my first test caps. As far as Jerome was concerned, well, I was just scared of him.

'Hika, you can do this but if they ask me who did it,' I told him, 'I'm telling them it was you.'

He begged me not to, so I relented and gave him a solemn promise that I would not. Hika spent the next 20 minutes drawing fairly heinous works of art on their faces while I giggled myself to sleep. When I woke up I saw Jerome's and Isaiah's faces. Not since Tame Iti has a face been so heavily tattooed. As I was staring at them in shock, they both began to stir.

I had a decision to make. A real team man would let a man know that he was about to disembark from an

FASHION & TANS

Hika Elliot was still laughing about the mokos two years later.

international flight with black ink all over his face. On the other hand, I had made Hika a solemn promise that I would keep his secret.

I did what any man in my position would do: I told them they better go wash their faces. And, as they got up to make their way to the bathroom, I added, 'Hika did it.'

For his part, Hika was now fast asleep and blissfully unaware that he was being ratted out three rows behind him. I was now in the clear with Jerome and Isaiah and, given Hika was slumbering away in front, I was surely clear with him, too. Unfortunately for Hika, he wasn't in the clear with Jerome and Isaiah, who decided to seek immediate revenge.

You should have seen Hika when the Immigration Officer in Hong Kong told him to go wash the giant permanent marker penis off his face. Lesson one: don't mess with Jerome Kaino.

I've long watched Jerome (from a safe distance) make massive tackles in test matches, but the one that will always stick in my mind is the stop he put on Wallaby Digby Ioane in the 2011 Rugby World Cup semi-final. It was probably the one hit that everyone remembers: Jerome picking up Digby and dragging him off the tryline and back into the field of play. It was a sensational tackle, and one that summed up the All Blacks' resolve that night.

I remember it better than most because it wouldn't have happened if I hadn't missed my own tackle on Digby 20 metres further back. Considering Jerome's legend was cast in stone with that one play, it's fair to say he owes it all to me!

9
ROOMIES I HAVE KNOWN

THERE IS AN AWFUL LOT to take in when you first make the All Blacks team and it helps to have someone you can rely on to make sure you are getting everything right. That man for me was Piri Weepu. When I first made the team I would text him constantly to make sure I had the right times for meetings and training and promotions. I was petrified that I was going to miss something and Piri was good at making sure I never did.

For all his qualities, though, you do not want to room with him. That man is a world class snorer, and Hosea Gear and Julian Savea are also in the snoring hall of fame.

When Julian snores it sounds like a pit bull choking on a chicken bone. I don't know what's going on there, but I'm never sure whether to throw a pillow at him or call an ambulance. It's a horrible feeling to be genuinely considering the prospect of having to give your teammate mouth to mouth resuscitation in the middle of the night.

The other annoying thing about Julian is that he is always on his phone. I don't know whether cellphone companies have got him on the payroll to check just how much a person can use one of their products before it explodes, but if he's not, he should be.

'Julz' and I roomed together in South Africa in 2014 and when I went to sleep Julz was sitting up in bed, on his phone. When I woke in the middle of the night, Julz was lying at the end of his bed, on his phone, and when I woke early in the morning, he was sitting on a chair, on his phone. And when I woke a little later he was finally asleep, snoring. On the floor.

Who stays up all night on his phone and then goes to sleep on the floor of his own room? We don't let Julz bring his PlayStation on tour now because if he does he's up all night playing it. The phone is bad enough.

There is one last thing about Julz: when he's in a grump, it's no longer your room, it's his room. Izzy Dagg felt the wrath of Savea in Argentina, when he got to his room to find it latched from the inside.

'Julz, let me in!' he pleaded.

'Nope, come back in five minutes,' came the terse response from inside.

'Julz, but it's my room, too.'

'Don't care. Come back in five minutes.'

ROOMIES I HAVE KNOWN

For all his qualities, you do not want to room with Julz.

And he doesn't just pick on the backs either. In Chicago that year, a few of the lads were in Izzy's room on the PlayStation when Liam Messam wandered in. He just took a seat on the bed and sat watching.

'Liam, what's up bro?' I asked.

'Julz is in a grump,' he said.

We all knew what that meant: he'd kicked Liam out of the room.

Anyone who knows me is aware I am probably the messiest guy in the team. I am the master of the 'floordrobe' so I always make a beeline for the bed furthest from the door because, if I don't, it'll just be a matter of time before the far side of the room is inaccessible . . . clothes, bags, gadgets, wet towels, assorted books, shoes and anything else that started life pressure-packed into my gear bag.

The All Blacks' long-term bag man Errol 'Poss' Collins used to hate to grab my bag because he was convinced that the slightest bump and everything would pop out like confetti.

If I'm the messiest guy in the team, Izzy Dagg is the smelliest. I don't get too close to him to quantify this assertion but, please, take my word for it.

Izzy is also a sucker for ritual and one of the worst is that from his shower, following the captain's run on a Friday, until the pre-match meal on Saturday, he has to wear his compression tights.

Now it's one of those unfortunate circumstances that

Not even the red nose can save Izzy from himself.

we are often put in the same room on tour and, aside from being smelly, he is almost as messy as me. That means there is always the danger of our clothes getting mixed up and, as any floordrobe aficionado knows, the only way to truly decipher the clean from the dirty after a while is through the age-old smell test.

The smell test is most often performed in an absent-minded, last-minute sort of way which, when you are dealing with possible clothing cross-contamination, carries a certain amount of risk. On one occasion I picked up a pair of compression tights off the floor and brought them to the nose for an olfactory investigation.

They were definitely not my tights. They were the

tights of the devil. Izzy thought it was the funniest thing he'd ever seen — me, almost fainting from the horrendous nasal invasion. All I could think of was his poor wife Daisy. That she has to put up with this man is one of life's great tragedies.

My kids have nicknamed Izzy 'The Bald Eagle', for obvious reasons. But even as his forehead grows by the day, he's still at me about my greying hair. I have reminded him on more than one occasion that I can at least dye my greys, but there's bugger all he can do about his shiny dome, but he still comes at me.

And he's now turning others against me. I'm worried about his influence over TJ Perenara, for starters.

TJ won't talk to me at training now, which is a very recent development. He's happy to have a laugh with everyone else, but he won't say a single thing to me while we're working on the field.

I'm starting to think that he's seen the end of my career coming and knows that soon he won't need me, so he's buttering up all the younger guys.

In Chicago, as I was hobbling off Soldier Field in the historic USA test, I saw TJ and Izzy wandering towards me on the field and thought, 'That's nice, they're coming to help their old mate.' Instead they started laughing! They then turned to the rest of the team and, in unison, said, 'F--k, he's old.' Damn near broke my heart that did.

Every time Izzy runs the ball back, his tongue is sticking out. You don't know whether to tackle him, or hand him

One day Izzy's going to run over that tongue.

a stamp. If he was able to run any faster the thing would be slapping against his cheeks. One day he's going to trip over it.

Truth is, Izzy and I have always got on, and neither of us know why. Well, he's immature and so am I and we both like to have fun, but apart from that, we've got nothing in common. I met Izzy through Zac Guildford on the 2010 Hurricanes' tour to South Africa. He and Zac had come up together through Hawke's Bay but only Zac had been picked up by the Hurricanes, while Izzy had to head south to the Highlanders. Both teams were in South Africa at the same time, and Zac introduced us at the team hotel.

Izzy told me that he didn't want to come to the Hurricanes because they didn't pick him as a kid out of school, the big sook. I had to explain to him that I was playing fullback at the time anyway, so there was little chance he was ever going to get that shot. It's fair to say we got on from the start. We have had plenty of mischievous adventures with the All Blacks, and a couple of decent blow-outs as well. But we'll get to that in good time.

More often than not the All Blacks management will put you in a room with someone who has similar tastes, and a similar disposition. Sometimes, though, you get a surprisingly different kind of roomie.

It was on just such an occasion when I found myself sharing a room with Ben Franks. Now if little brother Owen Franks is quiet, Ben is positively mute.

There are only two things that Ben wants to talk about: lifting weights and lifting heavier weights.

It's rare for a back to be put in with a forward on tour, but for some reason — maybe as a punishment for some training ground indiscretion — I found myself face to face with the big bear.

The problem with the Franks boys is not their personalities, it's their dedication to eating, sleeping and training. They're the only two guys I know, who after winning the Rugby World Cup final in 2011, went to the gym first thing in the morning. They could very well be the only two guys in the history of any world cup in any sport who have celebrated victory by doing 10 reps of 240 kilograms. Most of us hadn't even made it to bed by the time they were busy lifting whatever they could get their

A light workout for the Frank brothers, Owen and Ben.

hands on. Which brings me to the night in question.

I don't mind a man chucking tin. I don't mind a man setting up his own gymnasium in my room (and the Franks brothers both set up their own gymnasiums in their tour rooms; they have special weights freighted with the team kit). I don't even mind not talking for extended periods of time. But what I do mind is waking up sometime close to midnight to find Ben Franks deadlifting my bed. While I am sleeping in it.

Put yourself in my position: there you are having a good sleep when all of a sudden you wake to find a giant prop forward at the foot of your bunk going through 20 reps.

'Oh, hey, Ben. What you doing there, mate?' I asked in my most timid voice.

'Had to work out, CJ,' he grunted.

'Do you think you could work out with your bed, there, Ben?'

'Nope.'

'Ah, why not big fella?'

'Need the extra weight.'

I was the extra weight. It was bad enough having to endure three sets of deadlifts, but then he felt the need to do shoulder presses as well.

I was too scared to get out of bed and, anyway, considering I was suddenly lying at a 45-degree angle with my feet in the air and my head buried in my pillow, I was in no position to make a quick escape even if I had wanted to.

Mind you, I figured having him lifting my bed was preferable to having him want to jump in it with me.

I'm not entirely sure if any of the other boys have ever been used as human weights by Ben Franks. Perhaps they are too traumatised to say anything, even if they had been. But one thing is for sure, the whole team has been affected by Owen Franks' insatiable appetite for protein.

Kat Darry, our nutritionist, takes pride in making sure the boys always have enough to eat and drink on tour, and she's meticulous in her planning. As well as the normal stuff, the team goes through a fair amount of protein powder, especially after gym sessions and heavy trainings. Kat will stock enough protein for the week's training load in the team room, but you can guarantee by the second

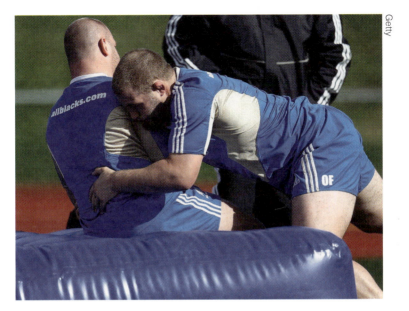

The Franks boys fighting again over a missing protein shake.

day it is all gone. And you can guarantee it has gone to Owen Franks' room.

I don't know what he does with it all, but I just picture him, sitting in his room in nothing but his undies, looking out the window vacantly, while spooning fistfuls of protein powder from a five kilogram tub into his mouth.

We all know Owen is the culprit, but I have only ever once challenged him on it. Not that it was my idea in the first place! I was press-ganged into heading up to his room one day to make some casual enquiries into the whereabouts of the missing protein supplies. Owen let me into his room and then proceeded to make himself a protein shake, with the aforementioned supplies.

'So, ah, does it taste good, Owen, all this stuff?' I asked, trying to break the ice.

'Nah,' came the articulate reply.
'Then why do you eat it all the time?'
'Because I get gains.'
'What? Like abs and things like that?'
'Nah. Just like smashing people.'

I let this sink in for a couple of seconds. I was face to the face with the beast, who I had caught red-handed, but now I was in a quandary: Owen knew that I knew that the product was there. He knew that I knew that he was using that product. But he also knew that I knew there wasn't a single thing I was going to do about it. Well, I thought, a man's gotta try.

'Do you think we could have some?' I asked, in my politest voice.
'Go get your own.'
'Well, Owen, you see, that kind of is the team's protein.'
'Nah. That's my protein.'

'Well, actually Owen, that's supposed to be for all of us.'
'It's in my room. It's my protein.'

Being a man of courage, a crusader for justice and a brave and tireless campaigner for the rights of the team, I thought about things for a minute or so and then I did what any other man would have done in that situation: I apologised to him for the interruption, said goodbye, and left him to it. Note to self: don't get between Owen and a meal.

Individually the Franks brothers are, well, interesting. Together they are a complete sideshow. They are the only two blokes I know who pack their own cooler bags every morning. They have all the food they need for the day — shakes, salads, vegetables, newborn babies — and they are extremely particular about when they eat it, right down to the minute.

One major hurdle when dealing with either of them is trying to decipher their facial expression. And I mean that to be singular. Pain, happiness, anger, distress, joy and despair have been reduced to just one look by the Brothers Franks.

Actually, I did once see Ben show emotion. It was while we were both playing for the Hurricanes against the Crusaders in 2014. I had put a (perfectly executed) chip kick over the rush defence and Blade Thomson had regathered and sprinted 40 metres to score. We were celebrating in the corner when all of a sudden Franksy came steaming in, chahooing with delight and picked me up off the ground. I now know what a salmon feels like, just before it gets eaten by a grizzly bear.

The boys couldn't believe it. This was a massive breach of Ben Franks protocol. This is a guy who is so concerned with the effects of dehydration that he won't even shed a tear.

This is a guy who has modelled his emotional range on the Terminator. I don't know what the boys were more excited about, Blade's try or Franksy's celebration of it!

The funniest thing was, he suddenly realised that he was smiling and enjoying himself so he dropped me on the ground and walked back to halfway. It was a glimpse, though — just enough to convince us that there might be more to the big fella than skinless chicken and weights. Afterwards, in the sheds, we gave him man of the match.

'I didn't do much out there, to be honest,' he said.

'No, Franksy. But the fact you joined a try celebration was enough for us!'

For the record, Franksy denies ever being involved in any such public show of affection. And none of us have seen him smile since.

Backs rooming with forwards is a rarity because it is just a stupid idea. We're not wired the same and everyone knows it. The most terrifying example of the folly of cohabiting the dumb with the restless came in 2012, when I was partnered up with Kieran Read.

Now, firstly, Kieran Read is another who needs to stop copying Richie McCaw's dress sense, though I suspect flared jeans and sponsor T-shirts are included in the All Blacks Captain's Manual.

Reado is a man who is taking his ascension to the throne very seriously, which is probably why everyone else takes him seriously.

I don't know if it was the chat about him becoming the next All Blacks captain, or if one day he just got out on the wrong side of the bed, but on this particular night during 2012, I was probably the wrong guy to be rooming with him.

Let me explain something here: I'm a bath man, and that's nothing to be ashamed about. A nightly bath is

Reado and Richie reciting the Captain's Manual.

the preserve of the highly cultured person. A bath is a refuge from the world of responsibility, a place to wash away the day and relax the muscles after the exertions of training. A bath is a personal experience, an escape from your children, a place to be buck naked and enjoy a soft drink. A bath should never be interrupted by a grumpy roommate. But while none of that is up for debate, Reado obviously never got the memo.

Suddenly, there was a knock at the door.

'CJ, I'm coming in,' came Reado's booming voice. There was nothing I could do; there was no lock on the door, and Reado sounded serious.

'Okay then,' I replied. 'But I'm completely nude and in the bath.'

I thought that would give the big man pause, but instead the door swung open and there he stood, glowering at me.

'What you after there, Reado? You wanna have a bath after me, mate?' I asked.

He just looked at me. 'It's bedtime, CJ, it's time to get out.'

Now, I'm a grown man, so the thought of another grown man telling me it was bedtime was strange. Even stranger given that it was just 7.30 pm. My kids are still up at 7.30. In fact, I don't even know if my kids are even home at 7.30.

'What are you talking about Reado? *Shortland Street*'s just finished!' I protested.

'CJ, it's a big day tomorrow and I want to get some sleep,' he continued. 'Bathtime is over.'

I have no problem with big Kieran putting his hands in the ruck, that's part and parcel of a loose forward's job. But, I have a major issue with him putting his hand in my bath. Before I could say another word, he plunged his big right mitt into the water, right between my legs, and yanked out the plug. Bathtime was over.

You can imagine the strangely dizzying state I now found myself in, but before I could gather my thoughts, Reado's throwing me a towel, and hauling me out of the tub. I'm thinking this is one of the great practical jokes of all time, but it soon dawned on me that this was a serious matter. It was like being cornered by an angry bull. I dried myself as quickly as I could and hauled ass onto my side of the room, which was separated by a sliding door.

I felt like I was in a movie scene in which the hero gets the door shut just before being overwhelmed by a horde

'CJ, just get into bed!'

of zombies or a swarm of bees. I caught my breath, sat on my bed for a few moments and then decided I'd use my phone. Ten seconds later, in he came again.

'CJ, get into bed!' he thundered. 'And I don't want any light either, so turn off your phone.'

By this stage I was seriously expecting to see 20 guys burst into the room, just like the big reveal on a *Punk'd* skit. Nevertheless, I turned off my phone and jumped into bed, as instructed. Then I turned the light on.

'Turn the bloody light off!'

So I did. And then I turned it on, and off again . . . and again . . . and again.

The big fella broke. And you know a guy is officially broken when he tries to kick open a sliding door.

'CJ, that's it!' he screamed. 'Get into bed and go to sleep!'

I'd had enough of this and I fired back. 'Reado, what the hell is going on here?' I demanded. 'First you yank me out of a bath, then you tell me to go to bed, now you're going completely nuts about the lights! What the f--k is happening here?'

Suddenly, he was a picture of calm. 'Nah, it's all good mate,' he finally said. 'We can just chill out.'

It was as if he'd just been exorcised. He turned around, sat down on his bed and took out his laptop. Slowly, as if I had just shot a rhino with a tranquilliser dart and was not quite sure it was fully subdued, I tiptoed across to his side of the room.

'So, ah, you're saying we can stay up now then?' I asked, completely bemused.

'Yep,' came the reply. 'I forgot I had to do these lineout calls for Shag.'

He then turned back to his computer and started making clips, and we never spoke of it again. I've roomed with Kieran plenty of times since, and there's never been a repeat. But just in case, I have a priest on speed dial.

It pays not to mess with the loosies, because they are all a little unhinged. They have to be a little crazy to do what they do on the footy field. And they are also big bastards, so you want them on your side if push comes to shove. Being perfectly proportioned (albeit in miniature) I have never been shy of making sure I surround myself with the real tough guys. When you have a mouth like mine, you can get yourself into trouble, so you have to have a plan for getting out of it.

Giant loose forwards are perfect for the role.

10
A LITTLE TOURNAMENT AT HOME

AS I'VE MENTIONED, once I became an All Black I set myself a goal of becoming at least a 50-test All Black. And once I had set my sights on the half century, another thought popped into my mind. It was 2008, soon to be 2009. The 2011 Rugby World Cup was not that far away. I decided I would have a new goal: to be part of a winning Rugby World Cup All Blacks team.

Manageable goals now keep an old man like me going, but back then they inspired the young boy within. I had gone from an eight-year-old kid scribbling down the names of the best goal-kickers in the country, and emulating them on the fields of Upper Hutt, to a 25-year-old kid standing on the fields of the world's most famous rugby stadiums and training with the next generation of stars.

Even in those seasons when things aren't clicking, your body is aching every week, and you are dealing with another setback, or non-selection or injury, having something tangible to work towards is crucial. It helps you deal with the inevitable slumps and hiccups that plague every athlete.

Having those goals makes you want to work hard, and you damn well need to work hard. There are so many amazing players, and there are so few guarantees when it comes to starting positions. It all comes down to millimetres at this level, and there have been plenty of outstanding players who, by virtue of being one per cent off the next guy, find themselves on the outside looking in. That is particularly true of the loose forwards, and it's certainly true of the back three.

At the start of the 2011 international season, for the first time in a long while, I began to have my doubts about whether I was going to make the grade.

The 2010 season had been good — a bunch of test starts and some really pleasing 80-minute matches — but 2011 just never seemed to click into gear.

I don't know whether the pressure was already building, at least subconsciously, ahead of the Rugby World Cup, or whether it was just one of those years, but the Hurricanes had an appalling season and my form was a long way off spectacular. I was watching the announcement of the team and they got to 'Kahui' and I was trying to remember if 'J' came after 'K'. My name wasn't called out in the team. Instead, I would come in as injury cover and would start the first test against Fiji at Carisbrook.

Some injury cover I was. That week I managed to suffer a compound dislocation of my finger, which didn't feel great at the time, and looked even worse. I battled through the week, but there was no way I could play a test match.

Ted asked me how I was, and I had to be honest (for a change). He told me not to worry, and that if I could get right in time I would start the next week against the South Africans on my home track in Wellington.

I immediately felt better. Up until then I had been so stressed about trying to rush back into action. In the All Blacks, we know that every game is an audition and every player is desperate to be named in the side each week. You are all in it for the team, but we're so competitive that we never want to give our mates a chance to outshine us.

The finger came right in that second week and, as promised, Ted gave me the start against the Springboks in Wellington. There are not many test weeks in which you feel perfect. Most of us are always operating below 100 per cent during a season due to the usual aches and pains and stresses the body suffers with the training and playing load.

That night, though, I felt unbelievably good. I ended up scoring two tries in a dominant team performance,

Happiness is scoring two tries against the Boks. Wellington, 2011.

A LITTLE TOURNAMENT AT HOME

and I think that one game, more than any other, may well have swayed the coaches to upgrade me from injury cover to World Cup squad. But I wasn't there yet, and as we were about to find out, there would be a very stressful morning, just around the corner.

That morning came for us after the Port Elizabeth test against the Springboks the following month. With another game in Brisbane the following weekend, and the Rugby World Cup now just three weeks away, the All Blacks coaches had to make the awkward call to name their tournament team in the middle of the Tri-Nations return leg tour to South Africa and Australia. They had no choice in the matter, and this was how it had to be; this was where we would find out whether or not we would be playing in the Rugby World Cup. If we needed any illustration of how cut-throat things were going to get, this was a fairly effective one.

We were told the night after the test match against South Africa that if we hadn't received a text by 11 o'clock the next morning, we were in the team. You can imagine us all sitting around waiting for the phone to ring.

It was probably the most nerve-wracking morning of my career. To lighten the mood, everyone was firing text messages at each other, though I think that did little more than ratchet up the tension.

I sat there thinking about my performance in Wellington, and hoping I'd done enough. I hadn't been picked for the following test, and had played just seven minutes in the losing effort to the Springboks the night before. Was my fate about to be delivered by thumb? There was nothing else to do except pace around the room and hope for the best. Due to the magnitude of the morning's decision we had each been given our own rooms the night before.

The deadline came and went, and my phone stayed silent. I've never been so happy not to receive a text from the All Blacks coaches.

It was great to be named in the World Cup team, but it was tough on the guys who missed out. Liam Messam, Hosea Gear and Wyatt Crockett had to travel on knowing that all the work they had put in to get their crack at a world title had come up short. I felt for them all, and I really felt for Crocky.

Wyatt is a great man on tour, but without Andy Ellis he's lost. Andy is known as Wyatt's tour wife, because he organises everything for him.

Wyatt basically wears him around like a backpack. It's a shame Andy can't do anything on the field to help his mate when it comes to banter, though. If there's one thing we are always telling Wyatt, it's that he needs to get some better chat.

On one occasion, during a test against the Springboks, the referee had separated the front rows to have a chat to Wyatt about his technique. Quick as a flash his opposite, Jannie du Plessis, piped up, 'You can't change the habit

Crocky: 'Hey, Andy, can you help me with the top button?'

of a lifetime, sir.' Now, you would think a man like Wyatt might have over the years developed an ability to throw a line back, but he just stood there looking hurt. In fairness, Jannie has a great respect for Wyatt as an opponent, just not as a comedian.

Not everyone can hold a comedy clinic at scrum time but Andrew Hore —when he wasn't hunting down New Zealand's coastal species — was a master at front row banter. I don't think he ever packed down in a scrum without dropping a one-liner. He also took his brand of Central Otago humour to rucks.

In one test against South Africa, Bismarck du Plessis had just got up from one ruck to head to the next when Horey, seizing his opportunity, yanked the big Springbok to the ground again. Bismarck was about to lose his rag

Even Woody's cracked a smile after Horey's one-liner at All Blacks scrum training.

but Horey just looked at him and said, 'Now let's be honest, Biz. Neither of us really want to go to that next ruck, so stop fighting this. I'm doing us both a favour.'

Then they cracked up.

There aren't many players in world rugby like Horey. I remember being told about a club game he played in after his retirement from professional rugby. Horey's local club is Maniototo in Central Otago, otherwise known as 'The Maggots'. Their home ground is called the Offal Pit. They had a game against Wakatipu and before the game the opposition coach made a point of warning his team to watch out for the great All Blacks hooker.

'Now look lads,' he told them. 'We all know Andrew Hore, freshly retired World Cup-winning All Black, is on the Maniototo side today, so get out there and give it all you've got.'

He paused for a second, and then looked at each of them seriously.

'But,' he went on, 'whatever you do, don't give him any lip.'

One of the club's young tyros, never wanting to miss a chance to prove himself, ran straight at Horey to start the game, and bumped him off! That should have been enough but the young buck couldn't resist a chirp to go with it. 'They reckon you're tough, mate,' he told Horey. 'But you've got nothing.'

'That's not entirely true, son,' Horey replied. 'I've got 72 minutes of footy left. Which is 69 minutes more than you have.'

Three minutes later, the young man was carried off. I'd like to say he will always remember his first game against an All Black, but I doubt he remembers much at all.

As most people know, Horey takes a certain amount of pride in his appearance and, after years of scrums, fights and rucks, he is now one of the few people who can listen to a conversation with his nostrils while he blows his ear. I took a whack on the face in a Super Rugby game against the Lions some years ago and when the doctor confirmed my nose was broken, the first thing I asked him was if I now looked like Horey. To my relief, he took one look at

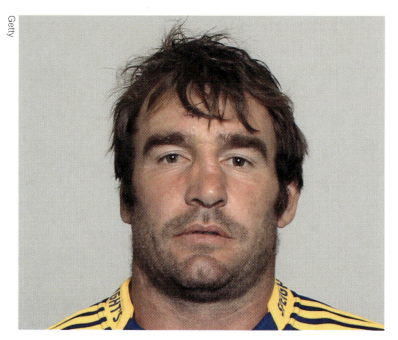

The famously frightening Horey visage. It took years of fights, rucks and scrums to perfect it.

me and said, 'No, mate, you'd have to work a lot harder to look like that.'

With the World Cup selections made, we could start thinking ahead to the tournament. I look back now and realise that none of us had any idea how big it was going to be. While each test is special in its own right, the nature of the busy professional season means the matches come and go, and the tours begin to morph into one. This was different. Suddenly everywhere we went there were All Blacks flags and banners and signs and people clambering to be a part of it.

You know things have got real when New Zealand's Tongan population ostensibly shuts down Auckland's motorway on their way to welcome their team to the tournament.

You just don't experience that sort of vibe in the course of an ordinary season. Everywhere we walked we could feel not only the excitement but the expectation. The opening game was a great occasion and for me a chance to soak up that atmosphere at Eden Park. We knew if we wanted to win the tournament, this was the place we would be doing it. Eden Park is great if you like big occasion test matches, and queues.

We played Tonga first up, and the Ikale Tahi were fired up for that opening match, and they really challenged us in key areas of the game. While the score blew out to 41–10 at fulltime, we felt we had been truly tested, and that gave us a base to work from.

Our goal was to get better with every game, regardless of who we played. And that's not easy in a tournament format where you come up against pool opponents of varying standards.

The next week we were in Hamilton to play Japan. I saw Brad Thorn had his own room, and I thought back to the night before my first test in Wellington in 2009 when he had suggested I go home and spend the night with my wife, considering we were in the same city. I remember thinking he was doing me a massive favour back then.

When I saw he had his own room in Hamilton, I jokingly asked him if he was moving up in the All Blacks pecking order.

'Brad here. Get me a room on my own!'

'I'm a bloody grown man with four kids, CJ!' he thundered. 'I don't need a roommate!'

Turns out he was rooming with Sonny Bill Williams, but Thorny had gone downstairs and paid for another room just so he could be on his own. Thorny was just like that, and it certainly wasn't a reflection on his roommates. I don't think so, anyway.

Thorny was not a complicated man. While the rest of us would sit in reviews and try to take in all the detail around running lines, and support play and body position, and option taking, Thorny always just wanted to go out there and push in the scrums and hit rucks. He was a soldier of a man.

A LITTLE TOURNAMENT AT HOME

I had come off the bench against Tonga in that World Cup opening match, but I got to start the Japan game, and we romped home. From there, it was back to Auckland for the pool match against France.

People always talk about how hard the French are to analyse and there's a reason for that: the French are damn hard to analyse.

We always look at France and wonder what they are going to bring. We had some moves cooked up to counter them in that pool match, and my try was off the back of just such a move. Regardless of the detail around move execution, one thing never changes in terms of our preparation ahead of a French test: we always plan to dominate them from the opening whistle. Whenever you play a team like France you have to get points early, otherwise you are going to be in for a hellish 80 minutes . . . and we would be reminded of that later in the tournament.

The weeks leading up to most of the four pool games were hard in some ways because we knew we were expected to win. There's a grind about the day-to-day work when you become so focused on perfection, but the ultimate result — with all due respect to Canada, Japan and Tonga — is almost a foregone conclusion.

We were all starting to feel the grind. And spending week after week in the same hotel was beginning to test a few of us. On the Thursday before the World Cup quarter-final, things would go a little pear-shaped.

11
A NIGHT TO REGRET

IT WASN'T THE FIRST TIME I had found myself in an embarrassing situation, but I don't think I had ever found myself in a *more* embarrassing situation, and I know I haven't since. My face, and Izzy Dagg's, splashed across the papers on the morning of the Rugby World Cup quarter-final against Argentina, and not for our teamwork in the back field. We would be in the papers for going out on the town. Not that either of us knew what we were doing.

Up until that point I think the most shamefaced I had ever felt was when Kurtley Beale knocked me out with a ball to the face in a Super Rugby match against the Waratahs. Actually, I still don't think I've ever lived down that grand falcon.

For some reason I thought it would be a good idea to

charge down a free kick but what I wasn't planning on doing was charging it down with my face. He dropped me like a sack of spuds, the little man, and I bloody hurt my knee when I fell, too, which made it even worse. I remember getting up and trying to run back into position — on the Waratahs side. Someone kindly turned me around and pointed me in the right direction. I ran past Rodney So'oialo and asked him what had happened.

'The ball hit you in the face,' he said.

'Don't lie,' I shot back, even though I had no idea what had just happened. Alby Mathewson was standing there laughing and backed up Rodders' claim.

'You got knocked out by the ball, you egg,' he offered by way of encouragement.

That week I got hammered in the review session: 'Where were you on this move, Cory?' I would be asked. 'What were you supposed to be doing here?' The answers to those questions were always the same: 'I actually can't remember any of it.' And for once in a review that was the truth.

I don't remember much about the infamous evening to be honest. Izzy and I had taken an extra sleeping pill before we had a massage at six-thirty that night — which was entirely our fault. If Doc Robinson had known she would have hit the roof. Pretty much the next thing I knew I was waking up in Piri's room thinking I had just enjoyed the best sleep of my life.

Not long after that, the shit hit the fan.

Piri didn't say a word to us, but he was the one who

came to find us the night before. We had gone out looking for some food by all accounts and ended up posing for photos at a bar. It was just so ridiculous. We went to training as usual that morning and, again, nothing was mentioned. It was only after we'd finished the session that we were called in for a meeting. We just assumed we would be in trouble for taking a sleeping pill, so we weren't prepared for what we were about to be told.

When we realised what a debacle we had created we were beside ourselves. Joe Locke, our media manager, had told us that it would be in the papers the next day. Ironically, that night I didn't sleep at all. I was so worried about what the media were going to report, and doubly worried because I had no recollection of what had happened. It's hard to call bullshit on the press when you're reading about your night out for the first time.

At 6 am the first stories came out, and the headline read: 'Jane Boozing'. To be honest, I thought it could have been much worse.

Wayne Smith, though, thought it was as bad as it got. Smithy is a massive culture man in a team and this to him was nothing short of a betrayal.

Our behaviour undermined everything he was working hard for, and everything the team had built over the course of the last four years. You just don't do that to Smithy.

The other coaches must have known that he would go on the warpath, because I don't think they told him what was about to come out.

Smithy's all smiles as I answer a question at a press conference two days before Izzy's and my night out. He wasn't so happy later in the week.

I probably could have done with a lawyer at this stage, but it wasn't as if Conrad Smith would be any help. After leaving me hanging on my first tour to South Africa with the Hurricanes, I knew he would never come to my aid in a crisis. I've spent years trying to make his terrible passes look good, but do you think he feels any need to show some gratitude?

Conrad is always smiling, and what a smile it is. He has teeth that point in every direction, allowing him to flash a smile at an entire circle of friends. Conrad also has the hairiest chest in world rugby, but he didn't get hairs on his chest in the weights room. There is not a player in the game with less love for the gym than Snakey, but he's always in there. And none of us knows why.

Well, we do know why: it's another place for him to whinge. That man can complain about anything. If Conrad Smith was in charge of modern music, you can guarantee a whole swag of hits would never have been recorded.

'So what you're saying, Meatloaf, is that two out of three ain't bad? Well, that sounds like horse shit to me. Two out of three is bad — it's just 66 per cent and, also, the word you're looking for is "isn't" not "ain't".

'Eminem, you can't "lose yourself", it's impossible. Go think about that for a while and come back to me.

'Well, I'm glad you never promised a rose garden, personally. Hellish things, roses. Thorns everywhere, hard to manage the pests. I don't see the point. Promise a "vege patch" next time, something useful.'

Conrad will whinge about anything and everything. He's spent so much of his career flapping his arms on the footy field that he's grown feathers on his biceps.

If he ever became a courtroom lawyer he would spend every trial objecting. All his career, people have called him 'smart', which he believes is a good thing. I keep telling him that he's only called smart because all the best adjectives were taken. But he objects to that, too.

I'm not saying an expert arm flapper has no place in the game. In fact, I think every team needs one. The issue here is that Snakey is relentless. He'll moan at training,

Above: Conrad Smith's 'hello world' smile.
Below: No one has a clue why Snakey goes to the gym.

he'll complain in conditioning games, he'll kick up a fuss on speed tests and he'll accuse everyone else of cheating.

I come in for my fair share of these wild and unfounded accusations. Almost every week he's at me about something; some perceived erosion of his moral high ground. And no matter how many times he comes at me, I always have the same answer: 'Well, Conrad, did I win?' At that point he usually picks up his toys and goes home.

Conrad has clearly stated that he will refuse to represent any of us, should we require legal assistance. Or maybe he said that he just won't represent me. Either way, I can't say I'm surprised.

He also has banned me from talking to him without an appointment at the Hurricanes. And when I do manage to pin him down for a chat, he charges by the minute.

Meanwhile, I knew I had to do the right thing by Smithy and also by everyone else in the team. I have never been so focused on a walk-through than I was the day of that quarter-final. Our shenanigans two days out were bad enough, but they were made even worse by the fact that the game also marked the hundredth cap for Mils Muliaina. The headlines should have been about him, not me.

Israel, who was rested for the quarter-final against Argentina, just said to me, 'Please, mate, can you carve up? Otherwise our tournament is gonna be over.' I was so amped up to make amends I could have played two games that day and I knew that I had to play out of my skin or

Doing my best to 'carve up' against Argentina in the RWC quarter-final in Auckland.

A NIGHT TO REGRET

Keeping calm with Piri.

there was every chance it might be my last game of the tournament. I did my bit for the team (and for Izzy's and my chances of a reprieve) and it felt good.

I clearly remember Ali Williams coming up and giving me a big sweaty hug after the game. He just said, 'Good on you for showing the world that the occasional blowout is okay.' Then he laughed at his own joke and wandered off. He was always laughing at his own jokes, but on this occasion I didn't mind.

After the game we apologised to the team in the sheds. Fortunately for us, Piri Weepu was about to knock us off the back page, having become the cult hero of the cup. The 'Keep Calm, Piri's On' T-shirts sounded a lot better than 'Jane Boozing'!

By the way, Old Piri pretends to be humble about that whole experience, but he was dining out like a boss on his newfound status as a goal-kicking hero.

They reckon the 'Keep Calm, Piri's On' T-shirt was one of the biggest-selling shirts that the manufacturer, Mr Vintage, had ever made. If you ask me, though, I reckon that's only because Piri ordered them all.

I'm telling you now, there are boxes of the things still stashed in a garage in Wainuiomata. We've all got one for Christmas from him every year since. And I swear I see the mayor of Wainuiomata, Ken Laban, trying to sell them to raise money for his council bids.

All joking aside, though, that was a tough time. When you read those kinds of headlines about yourself you understand that it's not just about you, it's about your family and all the people who have backed you along the way. Mum and Dad just thought I was an egg, which was really no different to what they usually think. And I'm used to disapproving looks from my wife, so it came as no surprise that she had one or two reserved for me as well.

Family, well, they forgive you pretty quickly. Smithy, however, didn't talk to me for a week. It wasn't until after the semi-final against Australia that he began to thaw. I guess getting through that game, the way we did, convinced him that we were completely focused on the job at hand. Smithy is pretty tough to upset so, in a way, knowing that we had really annoyed him was extra motivation for performing.

12
OLD FOES & MONKEYS OFF BACKS

WE WERE BLOODY EXCITED when we found out we would be playing Australia in the semi-final. They had beaten us in Brisbane just before the tournament began and we had looked forward to squaring the ledger at some stage in the World Cup. There was no fear as far as we were concerned, just excitement.

As part of the overall All Blacks build-up, the team was split into mini units and every unit had a specialist responsibility. Of course, that meant the Bomb Squad was back in business and Smithy was right into it. I had to remind him that Zac and I had already trademarked the name, and I asked him how much he was willing to pay to

The Bomb Squad: Izzy — you can just make out his shiny head — me and 'Kaks'.

use it. His reply was quintessentially Smithy: 'How about we pick you in the team?' he said. I thought that was a pretty good deal.

The boys were amped and for me that game was the most complete performance I have ever been a part of. Even though the scoreline wasn't huge, we started with a hiss and a roar and had an answer for everything the Wallabies threw at us. Wherever they attacked we had numbers on defence; wherever they kicked we had receivers. It is rare to be a part of a performance like that and it remains one of my all-time favourite matches.

The Bomb Squad boys were ready for everything that came our way, but, in truth, we weren't quite expecting the barrage we received. They put up a couple of high balls and we took them in and were able to set play. We thought after that they might change their tactic, but they just kept on coming. I could see what they were trying to do: it wasn't about contesting in the air, it was about allowing us to take possession so they could try to turn us over.

The fact we kept defusing the bombs, and gaining good ball to work with, coupled with the fact Australia just kept on raining them down on us, allowed us to turn the tables on them. We kicked, too. But the difference was they would take our bombs and we would turn them over. It wasn't the wrong tactic from them. It was a tactic that ultimately we countered — and countered well.

It was an interesting time for the team when the call had gone out to Beaver after injuries to Colin Slade and Dan Carter. I did mention to Ted that he might not have been aware of my glittering junior career at the Rimutaka club, when I had worn the number 10 jersey with such distinction.

'Piss off, CJ,' was his curt response. I don't think he was joking. You could tell the coaches were a little stressed out.

Whatever anyone thought of Beaver, the truth is, the man could play. When he arrived in camp we all said the same thing to him: 'Just do what you do, mate.' And of course, we all said it with a very deep voice because the one thing everyone who has ever met Beaver knows is that you cannot help but drop your voice a full

Ted considers the case for Jane at No. 10.

octave when you talk to him. He doesn't so much speak, he more rumbles. When he talks, whales strand. If Beaver was a musical instrument, he'd definitely be the bass.

He's a great guy to be around and, in some ways, the mood was lightened by his arrival. Destiny was set, time to get on with the job. He wasn't a pretty player, but he had a flair for the uncanny.

I remember once playing against him for the Hurricanes at Waikato stadium and he beat me with a bloody head step. His body didn't move. He just swung his head from side to side and still managed to fool me.

That was the sort of thing he did all the time. I was so embarrassed. 'Oh, CJ,' he said to me, 'I can't believe you fell for the head step.'

We just wanted to enjoy that final week. For us, the best teams are those that can back up their performances week on week. So many of the other top sides in the world can be mesmerising one week and miserable the next. Taking the dips and troughs out of the season had been a painstaking process for the All Blacks coaches. We wanted to be a team — needed to be a team — that could perform at or near our best every single time.

After the semi-final against Australia, we concerned ourselves with how we were going to repeat that level of performance. We all figured that the best way to do that was to release the pressure valve, which is easier said than done when a tournament is coming down to one last game. We were all sore, but there was little point in complaining about tight hamstrings when the skipper was walking around on a broken foot! We knew there would be no sympathy for the rest of us.

Piri was trying his best to stay out of the spotlight, having become the cult hero of the Cup. It was good to see him get some overdue credit, but the best thing you can do in a situation like that is to keep your teammate humble. That's what a real supportive friend would do, and no one was more supportive than me. I kept reminding him that he would soon come back down to earth and, sure enough, he missed his two attempts at goal in the final.

At a time like that, in the biggest match of his life, 'Pow' needed some encouragement, and I was there for him.

'See Pow,' I shouted from the wing. 'I was right. You aren't a very good goal-kicker.'

I was there for Piri when he kept missing in the Cup final.

Piri has always been a great team man. He comes from a fantastic family and they, in turn, are part of an incredibly supportive extended family which pretty much runs Wainuiomata. His brother Billy 'Big Show' Weepu was a fantastic rugby league player and is now a cameraman for TV3. Billy spends a lot of time working in Parliament, and it is said that he was once setting up for a press conference with the then Prime Minister Helen Clark when he realised he had left something in his work car.

Billy yelled out from the press row, 'Oi, Helen, you'll have to wait, I need to go get something'. No one else would dare talk to the PM like that, but this is a Weepu we're talking about. Sure enough, the Prime Minister agreed to wait!

'Come on Cory, one more game.' That became my mantra in the days leading up to the final. I just blocked out thoughts about the pressure and, in a strange way, I was probably more relaxed that week than at any other stage of the tournament. You could sense that everyone in the team was trying to get themselves into a similar head space, and when you are dealing with the demons and the doubts, you can't help but withdraw slightly. It felt like for much of the week the team drifted apart. We were still together, but the distance between the molecules had increased.

That bus ride to Eden Park on the evening of the final was unreal. Every street we turned into there were more people. Richard Kahui and I were bus buddies but I don't think we even talked. We both just stared out the window, amazed. We let the whole scene wash over us, lost in our own heads. It was a surreal experience, made even more so by the fact 'Kaks' didn't say anything.

The thing about Kaks is, he has no boundaries when it comes to privacy and that means no matter what you are doing, or what he's doing, if he feels like a chat, he'll start a chat.

Now, I'm a fairly open and relaxed kind of guy, but there are certain times when you don't need to be chatting, and when the bathroom door should be shut, and one of those times is when a man is sitting on the lavatory, as he was when he started this particular conversation:

'Cory, what was that move we had to learn for tomorrow?'

'You know the one, and close the door, man!'

'What? I can't hear you, CJ, you need to come closer.'

'I am not coming closer.'

'Don't be an idiot, get in here.'

'I am not coming in there, Kaks.'

'What's the problem, CJ?'

The problem is you are taking a dump, Richard.

He may not have an issue with privacy, but he is one of the most gifted athletes I have ever met — and bravest. Not many footy players would come back time and time again from shoulder surgery and immediately look for someone to put a hit on.

I don't remember much of the first half of the final,

Woody 'dunks the teabag' in the final.

which is why I am amazed no one has made a movie of *The Try*. Just imagine it! Ninety minutes of Tony Woodcock scrummaging and farming and five seconds of him scoring off a lineout move! Now that *would* be a box office hit. No dialogue required. (Also, I did not even get a mention in *The Kick*, so I'm a bit miffed about that.)

To be honest, I had no idea what was happening when that first try was scored in the final, though I did have the best seat in the house to watch it, as I was standing right behind the lineout. I had looked inside to ask Conrad what the move was and was ready to go when all of a sudden the lineout opened up and Woody 'dunked the tea bag'. None of us in the backline could believe the forwards had thought up something as beautiful as that all on their own.

About the only thing that stands out is Beaver running back after his penalty kick with his muffins hanging out the side.

He's a horrible man to watch at the best of times, but when he's on the big screen in slow motion it really is a sight you do not want to see.

I may not remember the first half, but I remember everything about the second. The French had come back with a try and, with the score at 8–7, we were about to go through hell. For 30 minutes they came at us. For 30 minutes we scrambled, and tackled, and somehow held our nerve.

I don't know how.

We were shell-shocked. At one point I turned to Izzy to ask him what the move was and he was as responsive

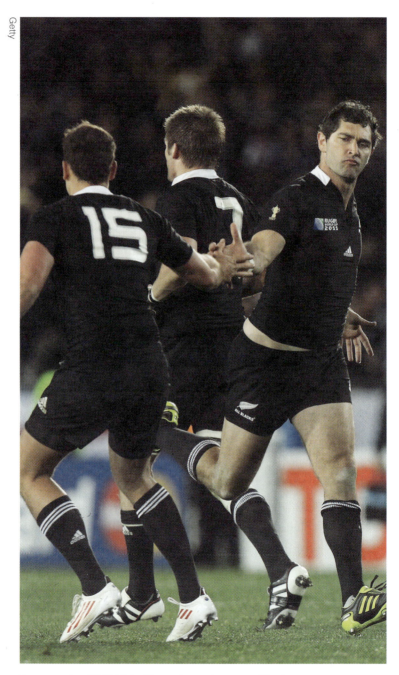

Beaver after THE kick. How about those muffins!

as a boulder, which is nothing out of the ordinary for Izzy, but I could tell he was mentally and physically exhausted. Richard Kahui was yelling at him from the other side of the field, but we were all borderline catatonic. Robin Williams should have been out there. It was like a scene from *Awakenings*.

After riding that team bus through a black sea of supporters on the way to Eden Park, we now realised that as much as we loved them, as much as they had shown us how much people cared, they couldn't help us win. That responsibility was ours alone.

Somehow, we finally managed to get our hands on the ball. There must have been 10 minutes left in the match, but at that point I knew we had won. It just seemed to me that after passing that sort of examination of our desire and dedication, we simply couldn't lose.

I got so excited about the thought that I even threw myself into the final ruck of the game — the first of my career — and when Andy Ellis kicked that ball into the stands, I yelled as loudly as I could, gave the world my greatest ever fist pump, and promptly collapsed in a dizzy spell. I don't know if the cameras caught it because I have never watched that game again, but if they did, I must have looked like a complete tool.

It was an amazing moment for us. We got into the sheds and drained a few cold ones and even the Skip was cracking jokes with everyone after that match! I had probably had six beers, which is more than enough for me, when media man Joe Locke told me it was time to go front the reporters. Lord knows what I said to them in my state but, having already made headlines for the wrong reasons once during the tournament, I didn't bother picking up a paper the next day.

13
A WEEK OF IT

HOW WOULD I DESCRIBE a typical All Blacks week? Well, the best way would be like this: you have seven days to do what you have to do to get yourself up for the game. Yes, there is structure and order to the days, but everyone has a different way of doing things in the spaces between.

MONDAY

Monday is a time to recuperate physically and be punished emotionally. It is recover and review day. If the boys are sore they might go to the gym for a light session or some time on the bike, but for us hard men of the team it's straight into the heavy lifting. These are the days I love hanging out with Owen and Ben Franks. After that we head into review . . .

I have spoken of the horrors of review already. After a win we expect to be singled out, but after a loss things are often short and sharp. That doesn't mean there is any less blood spilled, but everything is pared back in the wake of defeat — chat, banter, detail — the works. Everyone in the team has a chance to think about what they need to do to ensure it doesn't happen again.

The introspection is good. The problem could be as simple as a lack of discipline in line running, or a lack of physicality at the breakdown, or the fact you took your eye off the ball before you tried to catch it. We all know that by virtue of being in the All Blacks we are good enough as players, so it's about maximising our efforts in the game.

We're in the business of playing international rugby, and there will always be 15 guys on the other side of the field who feel exactly the same way.

We've talked about the game being broken down into moments, and the team being broken down into smaller parts. If everyone wins those moments and if every mini-team performs at their best, then you have to believe that you will come away with the win. But if you don't win the moments, and a couple of other guys don't either, or one part of the team fails to perform at its best, you are in trouble.

There has been a lot written on why the All Blacks have such a great winning record. For me, it comes down to the fact that we pride ourselves on being able to get up for every test match, no matter what team we're facing. We want to get out there and destroy teams — not by being cocky or arrogant, but by being focused, detailed and mindful of the legacy that we have inherited for the short time we get to play for the team. We are going to prove that no victory is a fluke. We are going to attempt to back up every win with another winning performance.

If you have any appetite left after the review session, it's time to grab a quick lunch with the team. Some guys pick away at a salad, others will engage in some good old-fashioned emotional overeating (whatever stops the tears). You can see them, tucked into a corner, eating bowls of ice cream.

The approach to nutrition within the All Blacks is certainly not as staunch as the regime imposed by Sir Gordon Tietjens in the All Blacks Sevens. Titch would take a sniffer dog on tour if he could, trained to pick up the scent of Snickers bars and red meat. Still, eating well is important in this business. After all, you are what you eat, I suppose. Which is why Piri looks like a cream bun and Andrew Hore is shaped like a beer can.

John Schwalger is probably the greatest eater I have ever met. He could devour five plates of food at a single

Super excited John Schwalger heads for the drive-through.

Sam 'Mono' Whitelock . . . the best eyebrows in the business.

seating. You always knew it was time to finish your broccoli and move on when Johnny started looking at your leg and licking his lips.

While food is always available at the hotel, over the last few years I have spent more time eating out. Nothing against the hotel food, but you do tire of eating in the same place all the time. Getting out in the evenings gives you a break from the monotony, and it also has another benefit: because eating out is at our own expense, none of the Crusaders ever wants to join us. You can always tell when a Crusader is about because their pockets smell like naphthalene.

You'd think that with arms as long as his, Sam Whitelock wouldn't mind dipping into his pocket, but I don't think I've ever seen it. I call him Mono on account of his one eyebrow. His eyebrow is that heavy he can't raise it without help from someone else. I'm reliably told that astronauts have now included Sam's eyebrow in their list of manmade things visible from space. Luke Romano must have thought the only way to get into the Crusaders was to copy Sammy, so he grew one, too, though he had the good sense to get his girlfriend to wax it. When they play together in the All Blacks now I like to call the second row our Morse code: two dots and a dash.

Sam may not be au fait with the requirements of facial topiary, but I will give him this, he's still the only man who can deal with a stomach bug by sitting on the lav while simultaneously throwing up in the bath.

I found that out on the All Blacks tour in 2012, when the team all went down with a virus ahead of the test against England. While undeniably gross, you couldn't help but be impressed with the man's efforts to responsibly deposit his waste.

Monday's the day to put the previous week to bed, so the rest of the day is used to free the body up, after the mind has taken its punishment. During a tour you have to be able to put things behind you and move on to the next task. Nic Gill, our strength and conditioning coach, has mellowed over the years. We first crossed paths when I was in the Junior All Blacks and he was as mean as a sergeant-major.

These days it's hard to argue with his methods — he

Nic Gill supervises another big weights session.

has been the brains behind our fitness regime for a long time now and his one goal is to make sure we are able to perform at the highest level, every week. Staff like Nic and Kat and all the other support personnel are just as much a part of the All Blacks' success as the coaches and players. They don't get anywhere near the credit they deserve, but we know how valuable they are.

Once we have finished our afternoon session we are free to spend what's left of the day getting set for the week ahead. We know full well that as of Tuesday we are fully focused on the next match.

TUESDAY

Tuesday is training day, and it's an important one. This is the day that the tone of the week is set. It starts, as every day does, with our 8.30 am meeting. Being a dad of four kids, I like to make sure I am up by at least 8.25. The country boys love to get up at dawn in the hope they can find something to milk.

Our Tuesday meeting is all about that day's training. You have to know exactly what you will be doing on the grass before you get there. That way you can put your all into the session without wasting valuable time on explanations. Tuesday training is the longest session of the week and will last up to three hours by the time the warm-ups and skills sessions are taken into account.

The Tuesday session is also probably the most physical of the week and that means the mouthguards go in and you are into your mahi! The idea behind the contact sessions is not to go out there and kill each other but, of course, there are still some guys who have only one speed.

Naturally you stay away from guys like Owen and Ben Franks, Wyatt Crockett and Sam Cane. Those guys don't know what the term 'body check' means. To them it sounds like 'body bag'.

As soon as the coaches call for a contact session you can see all the boys scurrying about trying to avoid having to form up with one of the training ground hitmen. It's probably the quickest any of us move during the session. Unfortunately the bloody fanatics are moving just as quickly to find the smallest guys in the team, so I seem to get stuck with them more than I would like.

Picture yourself, if you will, lined up no more than five metres from Owen Franks, and all you can see are his bloodshot eyes and the steam coming out of his nostrils.

Then you have to run at him. I'm not much of a religious man, but if ever there is a time I pray for myself, it is during one of these sessions.

I have first-hand experience of being crushed by my own overly competitive teammate at training. In February 2013 we were working through a touch drill with the Hurricanes. The forwards were working through their defensive detail around the ruck while us backs were looking at ways to get through the screen. I took a short ball from TJ Perenara and stepped inside the first man, only to be squashed by Ben 'Bam Bam' May.

Bam Bam is a ridiculously outsized human being, so it was never going to be a fair contest — especially when you're not expecting a full blown hit in a game of touch.

'Bam Bam' May. A ridiculously outsized human being.

I looked down to find my kneecap had been relocated to the inside of my leg, and my Super Rugby season over. Bam Bam was very contrite, but I still volunteered to take him to the airport when he signed for Japanese club Sanix at the end of the season.

When I found out he was coming back to the Hurricanes in 2015 I almost hung my boots up.

You can't blame the big boys for taking it all a bit seriously. Self-preservation requires a certain amount of intellect, and that's asking a bit much of them. But there is one group that takes it to the next level when it comes to being competitive, and that's the halfbacks. These guys have no off-switch at all.

The problem with halfbacks is that once they are on the field — whether for training or for a game — they think they are in control of everything. This is their time to feel special and you can't blame them, considering they spend the rest of the week requiring others to help them out with things like getting a glass down from the top shelf, or pushing the right floor button in the elevator.

Once they have their boots on, though, there is no such thing as 50 per cent. These guys are sprinting through their warm-ups, sidestepping people in walk-through drills, and generally pissing people off. They are the most competitive people in a team. TJ Perenara is so competitive that he once flunked an IQ test and didn't talk to himself for a week.

There is one upside to a halfback's competitive streak,

'You see, we're on the third floor, TJ. That's the one after the second.'

though: they refuse to let another halfback beat them. That provides the rest of us with hours of free entertainment. You can understand why they are so keen to outdo each other — the rest of the backline positions are a lot more interchangeable in the modern game, but there are only two halfbacks in the test team, and there's always three on tour.

At one stage in the 2014 season, Nic Gill lined the team up for the dreaded yo-yo test which, for those who don't know, is a particularly gruesome test of an athlete's aerobic endurance. The yo-yo was invented by a Danish physiologist by the name of Jens Bangsbo, who every athlete in the world wishes had done something more Danish, like making pastry or going for bike rides.

Needless to say, by the late stages of the test there were just three players left running: all three halfbacks, Aaron Smith, Tawera Kerr-Barlow and TJ Perenara.

And the only reason they were all still running was because none of them wanted to give either of the other two a chance to get one over them. The rest of us were watching on in hysterics, but each of the nines would have rather died of a heart attack than be the first to pull out. And they must have come damn close to having one.

Tuesday is a taxing day on the body and the brain, but Tuesday night is Club Night. All the boys pack their club jersey when they are preparing for a tour, and on Tuesday night we have an informal evening in the team room when the guys don their club jumpers, have a couple of quiet beers and a chip or two and generally throw around a bit of banter.

A WEEK OF IT

More often than not, there will be a skit or two on Club Night as well, and on one particular night, I had to don the number ones and act as club captain. My job was to hand out the fines for the week, and the first guy on my fine list was Shag.

Now, standing up in front of a room full of people is never my idea of a good time, but having mustered the courage, I called up the coach and ran through the charge sheet. Shag just stood there watching me. He knew he would have the last laugh.

'Righto, Shag. You were the one who dropped me last week so you can chop a beer for your sins,' I commanded. The boys all drew in a breath — they knew this was only going to go one way. Shag duly knocked the top off a cold one and no sooner had the last drop slipped down the gullet than he turned to me.

Shag always has the last laugh.

'I had no idea I would get a beer if I dropped you, CJ,' he said. 'If I get one every time I do that then you might be lucky to play another test.' And with that he just walked off.

The lads were in hysterics, and I had nothing to fire. I wasn't quite ready to commit career suicide, even if I had a decent comeback. It's a sport for Shag, part of his personality. He's always testing you to see how much you've got and that goes as much for off the field as it does for on it.

WEDNESDAY

Wednesday is a day to think of yourself (which simplifies things for Julian Savea because then he gets to treat it like every other day of the week) and for me it means a bit of a sleep-in. At some point Izzy Dagg will try to jump into bed with me because he gets bored and wants to go do something, and he knows the only way to get me out of my bed is to jump in with me. He's like a moulting Labradoodle.

This really is a day to switch off from rugby and do things that in some ways civilianise the week. Plenty of guys like to go shopping for their partners, though that's usually the new boys. Most of us old heads know that a big block of Toblerone from the Duty Free in Auckland will suffice.* Guys might decide to take in a movie or head out for a coffee or a bite of lunch. We have an option to

---

* No matter who you are, please know that this is a joke. The only person who will think receiving Toblerone from you is a lovely thought is your child, and even then they will still ask you where the toys are. Toblerone is a lovely chocolate, but nothing says 'You are an afterthought' like the gift of duty-free chocolate.

'Jeez, I wish I had hair like you, CJ.'

have a gym session in the afternoon, but in recent years we've organised a bit of basketball or some other cross-code hit-out instead.

The straight white boys from Christchurch — the Franks brothers, Wyatt Crockett and Sam Whitelock — like to get into the books and hit the computers. Walk into the team room on any day of the week and you'll be guaranteed to find one of them looking at clips on the PC. At least we think that's what Wyatt is doing, though there is a suspicion he's just Skyping Andy Ellis.

We do a lot of eating out on Wednesday nights. Julian, TJ, Izzy and I are always shooting out for a bite to eat, and mainly because it gets us out of the hotel, away from the intensity of the environment.

We're all relaxed people in terms of our build-up to the match so this is our way of jettisoning some of the pressures that naturally build over the test match week.

Also, the team appreciates me being out of the hotel for a couple of hours most nights.

When you are selected for the All Blacks, you are solely focused on the rugby. You can sleep in a hotel bed without being woken up (unless Ben Franks needs to chest press your bed, that is), you have the time you need to study moves, the food you want, the recovery time you require, and a support staff around you whose job it is to make sure you are at the peak of your powers come game day. For the dads in the team, your body feels great for not having been kicked in the crotch by a toddler for five straight mornings.

But, all that said, having a day to yourself is important — it allows you to get your mind off rugby and recalibrate the system. Tuesday is a big day on the pitch so your body enjoys having those hours to repair itself before you are back into it on Thursday. It helps, too, that Wednesday night is massage night, so it's the perfect end to any day.

Except, that is, for the one time in Japan when George, the muscle therapist, had arranged the local masseuses to turn up.

I was all set to have the full rub down when the lady started massaging my fingers. Then she moved on to my head. This went on for about 20 minutes at which point she told me she was done.

I walked past George on the way out and he must have seen the look of bewilderment on my face.

'How was that, CJ, does your back feel a bit looser?'

'I wouldn't know about that, mate, but my fingers and head feel fantastic.'

Turns out the 'masseuses' George had arranged were local beauty therapists, not muscle therapists.

THURSDAY

Thursday begins in the gym. This is clarity day for the boys so the gym is a wake-up call to get the body and mind right. For the backs it's a power session — light weights and explosive sets. We don't let the forwards in for this one as they have no idea about this sort of workout. They'd be standing there laughing at us, if they were allowed inside.

Thursdays in the gym — it's a forwards-free time.

We make them stay outside and get their lineout calls sorted instead, but we make sure we put all the weights back on the machines before they arrive in the gym.

If Tuesday is the big information day, Thursday is the implementation day. This is the day for putting everything into practice, for committing our moves to memory and perfecting them through repetition. Intensity is the mantra of the day. Everything done at pace, and done well.

By the time we get to the afternoon session we are ready for game-reality training. If you aren't prepared for it on Thursday, you are going to cop it. There is no time in this session to be studying your book or running around wondering where you are supposed to be or what you are supposed to be doing when you get there. You are expected to know your role and to perform it precisely.

I'm not one for books and computers, as you've probably already guessed. I like the unknown so I'll watch a little bit of the guy I am marking in order to understand what he tries to do and when and where, and then I'll form my game mindset about visualising the cues he uses. I think one of my strengths as a player is my ability to react to the changing dynamics in a game. I don't like to overthink things during the week because I feel it dulls those reactions on game day, and because I'm not used to thinking overly.

In the All Blacks you are encouraged to ask questions in order to learn, but that doesn't work for everyone, and it certainly isn't my go-to. I've always been a visual learner.

You can tell me something and I might get it, but show me it, and I'll rarely forget it.

Being a visual learner I could hardly complain about the guys I got to watch when I was making my way into the side: Joe Rokocoko, Sitiveni Sivivatu, Mils Muliaina . . . I would watch the lines they ran, where they stood on the field in different sectors of the game, and admire how they read plays and adjusted their patterns to account for subtle shifts in the game's dynamics. I try to do the same things today.

Thursday is a real business day for the All Blacks, so Thursday night is a quiet affair.

FRIDAY

The All Blacks obviously have a lot of commitments to sponsors and to fans, and Friday morning is a day to take care of promotional duties. The boys enjoy these sessions as long as they haven't been organised by Izzy Dagg.

I well remember the week leading up to the Argentina test in Napier back in 2014. Israel was loving being back in the Hawke's Bay, which he still calls home, despite turning his back on the province years ago for the greener pastures of Canterbury.

He was so excited about a local business wanting to help him out with a car that he had promised to take the potential sponsor out to dinner and, of course, he had promised the sponsor that he would be bringing Julian Savea and me.

Well, that's what he told us. On the night of the big date, however, things took a turn for the worse. And I knew they were going to as soon as he kicked me out of the bath — what is it with teammates bursting in on me in the bath?

'CJ!' he shrieked. 'Get out of the bath! We're going to be late!'

'Calm down, Izzy,' I replied, attempting to assuage the man's obvious anxiety. 'We're just going for dinner, mate.'

'Well, yeah, but we've got to go to Havelock North first, that's where this thing is.'

Now at this point my slow brain was starting to connect

the dots. All we had been told up to this point was that we were going to dinner with Izzy and a mate. Now we were going to 'this thing' in Havelock North.

'Izzy, I thought we were going to dinner,' I said, but this only served to fluster him even more. I didn't want him to lose any more hair over it but, by the same token, seeing the man squirm is just a great watch.

'CJ! We are going to dinner, we've just got to do a thing first. Now, where's Julian? Why isn't he ready?'

Suddenly Julz arrived in the room and for the next five minutes I got to sit back and watch him and Izzy go through the same routine. Eventually we started to make headway on the one thing that seemed to be missing: the truth.

'Alright, alright, you guys,' he finally offered, resigned to the fact that if he didn't fess up, neither of us were going with him. 'We've got to do a promo at the local pub, but you guys don't have to do anything, really.

'Oh and Shag and Shandy will be there and about two hundred people.'

Julz and I would have laughed if we weren't so angry with him. But one question still had not been answered.

'Alright, Izzy,' I finally relented. 'We'll go, but what about dinner?'

'I'll buy you a Subway on the way home.'

Only Izzy Dagg could turn a casual dinner out into a full-blown civic function and a takeaway sandwich.

Once promotional duties are done, we are off for our

captain's run. Most of the time this will be at the test venue, although Shag likes to sweep the area for spies and will often shift the run to another field if he suspects any prying eyes. I think he makes it up to have us believe what we are doing is so advanced it is a matter of national security and our solemn duty not to let any moves fall into enemy hands. Shag would have been great on the Manhattan Project.

'Look here, Oppenheimer, I don't like the look of that bloke in the hallway with the mop and bucket.'
'He's the cleaner, Shag.'
'Well, that might be the case, but I don't like the look of him anyway.'

The captain's run is a chance for us to familiarise ourselves with the venue, to get a sense of the occasion ahead of us, and to shake the last of the cobwebs out before game day. It's a light session but an important one. It is the one time in the week's training routine when the players take charge of what's happening on the pitch. It's a kind of cord-cutting before the test. After all, come kick-off time, we're the ones who have to control our destiny. A coach can't play the test for us.

It's also a chance to have a wee indulgence. After the run there are always treats waiting in the changing sheds: cream buns, cupcakes, caramel slices or something similarly immoral that would give the likes of Sir Gordon a coronary. Our former logistics man 'Poss' Collins instigated the ritual and Kevin 'Chalky' Carr, who

A WEEK OF IT

Shag's spotted yet another spy.

replaced him in 2014, has carried on the tradition. When Poss first brought them in, we all thought it was a trap, and no one was game enough to be the first to take one. It took several reassurances from the coaching staff before we all tucked in.

The calorie theme continues on Friday night with the chocolate run. It seems like such a school camp (or liberal prison) tradition, but every Friday night Chalky will come knocking with chocolate for the boys. Poss did exactly the same. You won't find an All Black anywhere but in his room at around eight o'clock on a Friday night because no one wants to miss out on their choccy bar!

It's ridiculous. We're grown men and we're all sitting there like junkies, staring at the door and moaning about Chalky running late with our fix! When he finally knocks on the door we know that's the last, sweet, full stop on the week.

On Friday nights we are all required to stay at the hotel — unless Brad Thorn wanted a room to himself. Quite often, if we are playing in New Zealand, the local lads will spend a few nights of the week at their own homes as it stands to reason that's where they are most comfortable. On the night before the game, though, we all stay together as a team.

GAME DAY

Apart from the odd exception, management are pretty good at putting each of us with similar personalities in the build-up to a match. I'm pretty relaxed, so the guys I room with are likely to be relaxed as well. After the captain's run a lot of the guys are straight into match mode, while others stay up late, and others like to get an early night. Friday nights you will always gravitate towards the guys who have similar ways of building themselves up, and the good thing is you can always find someone who is in the same zone as you.

I don't have a set routine on game day and that's the way I like it. Sometimes I will get up for breakfast and other times I'll have a sleep-in. I may have lunch, or I may have a nap. How I tackle the long day ahead of a test is dependent upon how I am feeling. There are plenty of guys, though, who have a routine that borders on OCD.

You get to know the guys' routines after spending so much time together, so you know who has to have breakfast early, and who will always be at the team lunch, and who will have to have a game of cards, or a pre-match shower, or an afternoon nap. Even though we all have a lot of banter, you never get into a teammate about his routine — it is his way of getting himself in the right frame of mind to go out there and do his job, and you need him to do his job.

I don't even mention Sammy Whitelock's mono brow on game day, even though all I want to do is give it a quick waxing.

You have to be especially mindful of the guys' routines if you are not in the playing team. If I am not selected that week but my roommate is, I'll make sure I ask about what he wants to do and when he wants to do it. That way I can make myself scarce while he gets done what he needs to get done. It's the only time during the week when I am not annoying everyone.

We have a final run-through that afternoon. It gets the team in the mood for the footy and takes care of the nerves that have been building during the day.

The walk onto the team bus is a time for each player to find his zone, whether that's with a book, or by listening to music, or simply by looking out the window on the way to the stadium. It's a surreal experience being on a bus with 40 other people while being completely in your own world.

A few years ago I decided I would try the book thing and so I started reading one on the way to the games. It's a good book and hopefully, in a few more years, I'll finish it.

I get excited when we get close to the ground and I can see the people outside, and I can visualise them sitting in the stands and watching me play. There are no more team meetings — from the moment we get on that bus we are charged with getting ready, in our own way, for kick-off. The individual routines continue once we're inside the ground. Some players do a lap of the ground, others like to stay inside, and some will need to be strapped if they haven't taken care of that back at the hotel.

Whatever works — that's the general rule before we come together as a team for the warm-up. That's the time you realign with the rest of the boys and get your body in the same shape as your mind. The warm-up is fast and furious and expertly planned. Before you know it you are back inside the sheds and awaiting the call to go.

It's about this time we are treated to what I like to call

the reverse peristalsis symphony. Nothing says you're about to play a test match like listening to half a dozen of your teammates throwing up in the cubicles. Don't ask me why they do it, but it gets me every time.

There are very few words required in those final minutes. If you have nothing to say, you don't say anything. Richie will remind us of some key points that we have focused on during the week, and if there is anything else, the game leaders will chip in. But, in reality, the time for talk is well finished.

That didn't stop Dane Coles taking us back to the old school in South Africa early in the Hurricanes' 2014 season. Colesy had been given the captain's armband after Conrad Smith had travelled back to New Zealand early and he was a bit nervous during the week about how his pre-match speech would go. All week he was at me: 'CJ, you have to help out, mate, you're one of the leaders and I need you in there!' I, of course, reassured him that everything would be fine.

We got to game day and as we came in for the huddle, we all waited for the final words of wisdom from our new leader. He looked around the room and then, like a Labrador that's just seen a tennis ball, he delivered the most inspirational message in the history of the game.

'Okay, guys . . . ah . . . let's go out there and . . . AND WASTE THESE F--KERS!'

Dane Coles . . . a man who knows how to inspire.

It wasn't the words so much as the fact his voice broke halfway through, but regardless, I did something I had never done in a pre-match huddle, and burst out laughing. Most of the team were giggling as we ran out onto the field. We got the win that day all the same, and after the game Colesy had a good laugh at himself as well.

I don't sing the anthem, and I get asked all the time why that is. Actually, I used to. Then one day I stopped and heard all the other guys singing, and thought if it sounds this bad already, the last thing it needs is my voice!

In truth, the first time I heard all the other boys singing it really fired me up, and I realised that when I was singing along, I wasn't hearing them. So I stopped, and listened, and focused on someone in the stands in an All Blacks top, and I loved it. And that's what I have done every time since: listened to the boys, and the crowd, and looked directly at an All Blacks fan in the crowd. It could be you, you know.

Of all the things that I love about being in the All Blacks, performing the haka has to be the one thing I love the most. Being a small, white boy I just make my way to the front and get as staunch as possible. I always try to find my opponent and stare at him while I am laying down my challenge. That's what gets me going the most.

I feel bulletproof after the haka, I really do. And when that opening whistle goes, the fun part of my week begins. That's when I get to be six-year-old Cory again, just playing the game with a bunch of my mates, and loving every second. Six-year-old Cory, the kid who told anyone who cared to listen that one day he was going to be an All Black.

EPILOGUE

EARLY IN 2015, Wayne Smith and I were standing in a small meeting room at Hurricanes HQ in Wellington. Smithy had agreed to rejoin the All Blacks coaching team for the 2015 Rugby World Cup and was on a tour of the franchises, talking to a few of the players.

Smithy is what you might describe as a very spiritual person, in the sense that he is always trying to divine what is inside you; whether the personal spirit for the game is residing within you. When he gets into his spiritual detective work, it can be a fairly unnerving experience for the player under investigation.

'Stay still, CJ,' he said to me. 'I'm trying to look into your eyes to see if the glow is still there.'

The last time he had asked me a question like that was in my first year with the team.

'Don't you worry about that, Smithy,' I responded, staring straight back. 'That glow is there alright.'

It was a timely reminder never to take this job for granted. You have to have the desire and the passion and the commitment to want to play international rugby. And you have to have the spirit to want to get better.